THE ORCHID WHISPERER

THE ORCHID WHISPERER

EXPERT SECRETS FOR GROWING
BEAUTIFUL ORCHIDS

Bruce Rogers

Photographs by Greg Allikas

CHRONICLE BOOKS
SAN FRANCISCO

Library of Congress Cataloging-in-Publication Data:

Rogers, Bruce, 1952–
        The orchid whisperer : expert secrets for growing beautiful orchids /
    by Bruce Rogers ; photographs by Greg Allikas.
            p. cm.
        Includes index.
        ISBN 978-1-4521-0128-6
        1. Orchid culture. 2. Orchids. I. Allikas, Greg. II. Title. III.
    Title: Expert secrets for growing beautiful orchids.
    SB409.R64 2012
    635.9'344—dc23
                        2011020708

Manufactured in China

Designed by Supriya Kalidas

Photo Credits:
pg. 110: istockphoto.com/chrisgramly
pg. 112: Janis Christie/Photodisc/Getty Images
pg. 119: Thinkstock/Comstock Images/Getty Images
pg. 124: istockphoto.com/arekmalang
pg. 127: istockphoto.com/dulezidar

10 9 8 7 6 5

Chronicle Books LLC
680 Second Street
San Francisco, California 94107
www.chroniclebooks.com

DEDICATED TO MY FAMILY —

Jan, Alexa, and Nick.

CONTENTS

INTRODUCTION

Truth be told, I did not set out to write a book called *The Orchid Whisperer*. But my editor knew I already had the moniker and felt it would be a good title, so I decided to run with it. (Plus, I liked the idea of creating an orchid book that is around the same retail price as a regular orchid). I have been growing and decorating with orchids for thirty years and the reality is that the more time you spend with orchids the better you get to know them. Now I'm sharing what I know in this book.

Growing up in Berkeley, I spent quite a lot of time in the garden. When I was about twelve, my grandmother announced that I had a way with plants, just like her father who was a respected Russian naturalist and paleontologist. By my middle teens, I was working after school as a gardener. It was in these gardens that I discovered my first orchids.

In my early twenties, a job opportunity to work as an orchid consultant for the city of Atlanta presented itself. A fancy title, but in reality it was more about repotting, cleaning the orchids, and establishing some sort of regular maintenance schedule. I was very lucky—when I left, all of the orchids were blooming their heads off and I had great letters of recommendation in hand. I returned to San Francisco and was hired by the Rod McLellan Orchid Company (one of the very best firms at the time) as the head of their orchid-boarding department. It was my dream job.

After a while, wanting more of the orchid world, I left the firm and several of my major clients asked if I would keep them on. Of course I agreed, and from there I was able to form my own orchid maintenance, sales, and boarding business.

I started supplying interior decorators and worked to get orchids into major hotels, restaurants, and department stores. It was an exciting time. I selected and maintained the orchids for the famous Compass Rose Room at the St. Francis Hotel in San Francisco. I did the orchids for Saks Fifth Avenue, who kept their orchids on the design and couture floor, and I was in charge of the orchid program for Nordstrom, had my retail orchid shop at the old Gumps store, and rented orchids to both Ralph Lauren Polo and Hermès of Paris. I also planned special orchid events for fashion shows and big firms like Cartier. During this period I was exposed to an incredible array of orchid growing and display situations, at every economic and social level.

I also had private clients who hired me to manage their personal orchid collections and do the orchid design work in their homes. I continue to do this to this day—I've had some of my clients for over twenty years! This has been fun, exciting work, allowing me to hunt for orchids in the jungle (which is really awesome, especially when you're getting paid for it), attend auctions for luxurious containers for displays, and have the freedom to express my creativity in my clients' homes.

I don't know if all of this qualifies me as an orchid whisperer. I do know how to grow orchids— one client likes to claim that I can make a brick bloom—and I share the tricks I've learned over the years in these pages.

The book starts out with a handy visual glossary to familiarize you with the important terms and parts of the plant before getting started. From there, you will learn how and where

Beautiful, easy-to-grow phalaenopsis, with their long-lasting flowers, are a beginner favorite.

to buy orchids (that big-box chain might actually be your best bet); which are the top twelve most popular orchids and what you need to know to grow them; how to care for your orchids so they bloom again and again; and, finally, how to display and decorate with orchids.

I wrote this book primarily with the goal of helping the beginner realize that growing orchids is like having a pet or a child: If you pay attention and provide for their needs, they will repay you with love. I also hope to take the fear out of orchid growing. Even if you've failed to bloom an orchid in the past, don't worry. There are hundreds of tips included here to help you keep your orchids blooming, no matter your experience level, budget, location, or environment. But the main thing I hope you learn is that growing orchids mimics life: the more energy you put into it, the more you will receive.

GLOSSARY

AERIAL ROOTS / Roots growing in the air at the base or stem of an orchid, absorbing water and nutrients from the air and also acting to physically support and secure the orchid in its habitat.

BASE / The bottom of the orchid plant, just above the underground root system.

BULB / A ball-shaped growth above the underground roots, and below the top leaves in orchids such as oncidiums. This is where the orchid stores nutrients and water.

CANE / The elongated stem-like growth that holds a flower spike in orchids such as dendrobiums.

CROWN / The top of the leaf section of an orchid, where new leaves grow.

DORMANT PERIOD / The time period when the orchid is resting and not actively growing or blooming.

EPIPHYTIC / Orchids that grow on other plants or objects, taking their nutrients from the air. Common for orchids that grow above ground.

FLOWER NODE / The place where a flower joins a flower spike.

FLOWER SHEATH / A leafy tissue that surrounds an emerging flower spike.

FLOWER SPIKE / A stem that carries flowers.

GENUS / A named category of orchids that are similar either in appearance or DNA structure; the category just above species.

GROWTH PERIOD / The period of time where the orchid is actively growing new roots and bulbs.

HYBRID / The progeny of two different species, genera, or hybrids.

KEIKI / A Hawaiian word meaning "baby" or "little one," used to describe new plantlets that form either on the flower spike (with phalaenopsis, oncidiums, and epidendrums), on the old canes (dendrobiums, epidendrums), or at the top of old bulbs (Australian dendrobiums).

LIP (A.K.A. LABELLUM) / A highly modified petal where the column and anther of a flower are found.

MONOPODIAL / A term that refers to a single-stemmed orchid, which grows from the terminal bud at the apex or culmination of the plant.

NODE / The place where a leaf joins a stem or bulb, defined by a line circling the stem or bulb.

OVARY / The ribbed section at the top of the flower stem and behind the flower that becomes a seedpod after pollination.

PETALS / The modified and usually brightly colored leaves that surround the reproductive parts of a flower.

PSEUDOBULB / A thickened or swollen stem that has a bulblike appearance but is not a true bulb. Stores nutrients and water.

RHIZOME / A stem, often horizontal, that forms roots rather than leaves, usually underground.

ROOT / The part of the orchid that bears no leaves and draws food and water into the plant from the surrounding environment. Generally terrestrial orchids have underground roots and epiphytic orchids have aerial roots. The underground roots should be visible at the base of the plant, as the base is not buried in the potting medium—this is where new roots will emerge and the new tips can be seen before growing down into the potting mix. You can also brush away the potting mix by the bulbs to peek at the roots.

SEEDPOD / A capsule-shaped fruit containing seeds.

SEPALS / Modified leaves that enclose a flower before it blooms and then become the lower part of the blossom, under the petals.

SHEATH / A leafy, sometimes tubular structure surrounding any orchid part.

SPECIES / A group of orchids found in nature that share common characteristics and DNA.

SYMPODIAL / A term referring to multistemmed orchids, which seasonally produce one or more new bulbs at the base of the plant.

TERRESTRIAL / Orchids that grow on the ground with their roots in soil.

A phalaenopsis hybrid will bloom for months given ideal conditions.

Part One

BUYING ORCHIDS

FIRST THINGS FIRST: BUY WHAT YOU LIKE!

When shopping for orchids, take a look at all the different kinds available, and choose the one or ones that appeal to you most. Don't worry about whether you can get a particular orchid to bloom. I promise you that you can do it. I know orchid novices who bought notoriously difficult-to-grow orchids, only to have them bloom again and again. I believe that when you choose an orchid you like, the success rate for growth and repeat blooms is much higher than if you choose an orchid just because someone says it is easy to grow. Besides, this book will help you grow healthy orchids that bloom repeatedly.

Before you buy an orchid, be sure to get its name. If there is no name tag, ask the salesperson. It is very important that you know what type your orchid is, so you can learn to care for it properly. Also, ask for growing tips, especially when buying directly from the grower, as growers are a great resource.

A cart full of cattleyas

What to Look For

Buying a healthy orchid is the key to the plant's longevity. Beginning orchid growers may have a hard time spotting the important physical qualities and faults of individual plants, so here's a handy checklist to help you select a healthy orchid.

THE FLOWERS

❖ Once you have selected the kind of orchid you want, look at the other orchids of the same type and compare the flowers. Some plants may have larger flowers and more abundant blooms than others. These are generally the healthiest.

❖ Look at the unopened flower buds. All flower buds should be green (not yellow) and graduated in size, from largest at the bottom to smallest at the tip of the flower spike. The more flower buds a plant has, the longer the flowering time for the plant, which means more flowers to enjoy. Avoid any plants with yellowed and shriveled flower buds or missing flowers.

❖ Examine the flower spike (the stem from which the flowers bloom) at the spot where it emerges from the plant and check to make sure it is not bent. A bent spike can impede a flower's longevity. Check to see if the flowering spike is branching or beginning to branch, which indicates that the plant is healthy and will continue to produce more flowers.

❖ If you are looking for a fragrant orchid, smell flowers from different plants. Even among orchids of the same type, some can be more fragrant than others. Remember, not all orchids are fragrant, and many are fragrant only at certain times of the day, so be sure to ask about this before purchasing. (For a list of fragrant orchids, see page 137.)

THE PLANT

❖ Next, look at the orchid plant itself. Go ahead and pick up the plant to see if it wobbles around in its pot when you move it. The plant should be rooted well enough that it doesn't wobble, because if it's loose inside the pot, this means that the root system has failed. This is a serious problem, as it has to re-establish itself. A plant in this state will not bloom properly.

❖ The orchid plant should have healthy looking, undamaged green leaves. Orchid leaves naturally grow in different shades of green, ranging from pale to dark green. The pigment should be evenly distributed on the leaf, that is, the color should be solid, with no yellow blemishes. Yellow leaves usually indicate that the plant has received too much sun and is damaged. Leaves should be self-supporting, not limp or held up with plant stakes. There should not be any black or brown spots or streaks on the leaves. Avoid leaves with black tips; this usually indicates root problems.

❖ The more leaves the better, as this indicates that the plant is older or, if you are lucky, that the pot contains more than one plant.

THE BULBS

❖ If the plant has bulbs or pseudobulbs (meaning it is a sympodial, or multistemmed orchid such as a oncidium (see page 75), they should be nice and plump, especially the new-growth bulb that holds the flowers. Bulbs and pseudobulbs, which are above the surface of the pot, are where the plant stores water and nutrients. Plump bulbs mean that the plant is hydrated. The more bulbs, the better—this indicates a more mature plant. Monopedial, or single-stemmed orchids like phalaenopsis (see page 60) don't have bulbs or pseudobulbs, but they may have multiple growths in the pot, each one a separate plant. If so, you will be able to later divide the growths and pot them separately.

BUGS AND PESTS

❖ Look carefully at the flowers and peek underneath the leaves and in the crevices of the bulbs to check for any critters. If you find any spider-like bugs on the flowers or new growth; mealy bugs (which look like white cottony fluff); black or white bugs on the leaves or plant itself; or any holes in the flowers or leaves, that orchid has a problem. (See page 44 for more information on pests and diseases.) No matter how much you want an orchid, do not buy it if you find that it has pests. I have done this in the past, only to end up spending weeks or months waging an unsuccessful war against them. I don't recommend this approach.

BUYER BEWARE

It's sad but true: some sellers try to disguise faults in their orchid plants. Here are some tricks to watch out for:

❖ **BROKEN FLOWER SPIKES**
It's common for sellers to hide a broken or bent flower spike by adding a stake for support. This is especially a problem with taller orchids. Because most orchids have tough, fibrous flower spikes, when a spike is broken or bent badly, it may not split or break off, but the damage will affect the flowering.

How to Spot / Look for unnatural-looking bends in the flower spike. If you find one, check how the spike is attached to the support stake. The big tip-off is if more than two attachment wires are used to tie the flower spike to the stake. If you are looking at a tall orchid that is tied to the support stake more than five times, I would definitely take a closer look to see why the spike needs so much support.

✤ A SICK PLANT

When an orchid's root system has failed or the plant has been damaged by insects, viruses, or sun exposure, the plant starts to dehydrate and the tips of the leaves begin to turn brown and die. Some sellers just trim off the brown parts of the leaves and sell the plant anyway. Because of this, a damaged plant can be hard to spot.

What to Look For / Leaves should be a natural oval shape. Examine the edges of an oddly shaped leaf: If it looks cropped off, it could mean that someone has trimmed the leaf to remove spots or damaged areas. Also, look for an unnatural absence of leaves, which likely means the seller has removed all of the unhealthy ones. Stay away from plants with leaves that have black streaks or discolored rings, both signs of a virus. Examine the flower; if the coloring is streaked or blotchy, the plant likely has a virus.

✤ A PLANT IN THE WRONG SIZE OF POT

It is common for sellers to transfer flowering plants from pots that are too small for them and stuff them into a larger pot rather than repotting the plant. Usually this is done because the plant became top-heavy from the foliage and could no longer stand on its own. An easy solution is to shove it into a larger pot and cover the top with potting medium (sometimes even leaving the plant inside the smaller pot and just burying the smaller pot under the potting medium). But since the root-ball is not integrated with the new potting medium, rot quickly appears. (For more on repotting, see page 30.)

What to Look For / Brush away a little of the potting medium at the top close to the plant to make sure the medium below is of the same texture and color. If not, or if you uncover a smaller pot inside the larger one, immediately ask the seller what is going on.

✤ ADDED FLOWERS

It's hard to believe, but some sellers add cut flowering spikes to existing plants to get a higher price. They insert the flower spikes in small floral tubes of water to keep the flowers fresh, pushing the tubes into the pot until they are concealed from view.

What to Look For / Follow the stalk of the flower spike down to its base, where it should be attached to the plant. If it disappears into a plastic tube stuck into the pot, find yourself another orchid or ask the seller to lower the price.

What to Ask

When you have determined that the orchid you have selected is healthy, be sure to ask the salesperson the following questions:

✤ *"How long do these flowers last?"* Orchid flowers can last from one day to a couple of months, depending on the orchid type. You want to be prepared for what is normal for your particular plant.

✤ *"Is this flower fragrant?"* Ask this even if you can't smell a thing; many orchids are fragrant at different times of the day and night, and the answer may influence your decision to buy the orchid.

✤ *"How big does this orchid get?"* This question is not asked often enough. Some orchids can grow really large. That little 10-inch orchid you're buying might be 4 feet tall in two years. You need to know this ahead of time.

Where to Buy

The orchid market has changed dramatically in the last twenty years as orchids have become the world's favorite houseplant. With the infinite number of types of orchids and their growing needs, no one company can grow everything. There are many different places to look for orchids, from supermarkets to orchid societies, and each has its own benefits and challenges.

LOCAL ORCHID SOCIETIES

Your local orchid society is the ideal place to buy your first orchid. No matter where you are in this world, you are not far from an orchid society or club (see "Resources," page 131). Orchid society meetings, usually held once a month, are friendly gatherings and a great resource for the beginner. These people are really into orchids and will be happy to teach you a thing or two. All meetings have a sales table where members sell their extra orchids, and prices are very fair, with bargains being the norm rather then the exception. (Note: Some societies require you to join before you can buy plants, so be sure to ask ahead of time.)

During the meeting, members talk about the orchids they've grown and brought for show and tell, which is always informative. Meetings usually also feature a talk from a guest speaker on various topics. If you do want to join, orchid society membership fees range from $10 to $40 a year, and there are no attendance requirements, although some societies may ask that members supply snacks once a year.

ORCHID NURSERIES

Orchid nurseries are wonderful for orchid beginners. At nurseries, you will find an exciting selection of orchids and all the help and answers you need. Orchid nurseries are found all over the world, from huge ones open seven days a week to mom-and-pop operations (see "Resources," page 131).

Beautiful vandas at a nursery in Florida. Note the healthy vanilla orchid vine in the left foreground.

The advantage of specialized nurseries is that the growers are passionate about orchids. At a nursery, you can see orchids in their ideal growing environment. Be sure to walk around, check out the greenhouse, and ask questions. This is an opportunity to learn where specific plants are from and what they need in order to bloom. Orchid prices are reasonable, as the growers want you to return.

ORCHID SPECIALTY STORES

Many major cities now have stores that sell orchids exclusively. Generally, these stores offer both commercially raised orchids and plants from local hobbyists. The staff is trained specifically in orchids, which can be a great resource for the beginner looking for help. These shops have high standards for their orchids, so their plants tend to be very healthy; they are also stocked with the best orchid-growing supplies, containers, and mosses, which makes them great for one-stop shopping. The downside is that their prices tend to be high.

GARDEN CENTERS AND PLANT NURSERIES

Many garden centers and plant nurseries carry orchids, especially those that can be grown outside in a particular region. Plant people can be a little more in touch with orchids than the sales help at your local supermarket, but these people are not necessarily orchid experts. Plant nurseries also tend to sell orchid supplies, and are a good resource for products such as bark and perlite (a common soil additive), both useful in growing orchids (see page 31 for more information). Unfortunately, not all plant nurseries carry orchids, so be sure to call ahead. Unless they have grown the orchids themselves, they have purchased the orchids elsewhere to be resold, and prices will reflect this.

FLORISTS

If you live in a small town or rural community, your local flower shop might be your only choice for finding an orchid. Because orchids are such a traditional gift flower, all florists have some access to orchids and usually have flowers and plants shipped in, so bargains are harder to find. But in smaller towns, florists are sometimes the only sales outlet for local orchid growers, which means that jewels can be found. I always stop in at any florist I see to check their orchid selection.

FARMERS' MARKETS AND FLEA MARKETS

Farmers' markets are a source of both poor- and high-quality orchids, so first-time orchid buyers should be on their guard here. There are two types of sellers: the orchid grower, who grows and sells his or her own orchids, and the orchid middleman, who buys plants wholesale to resell them. Orchid growers use this outlet to sell larger orchids that cannot be shipped and sometimes, unfortunately, to sell inferior or weak orchids that they do not wish to sell at their nurseries. Orchid resellers generally look for the most attractive plants available, but sometimes, with only the best price in mind, they will buy and resell orchids that are hard to grow or do not bloom regularly, or worse, that have viruses or pests. Use your buying skills and check each plant carefully before purchasing. Prices tend to be normal retail.

Flea markets are really the Wild West of orchid sales, and are not recommended for the orchid novice. I have seen everything at flea markets from orchids in ornamental pots obviously stolen from some front porch the night before to flowerless plants that don't have a chance of blooming for three years to plants that will be dead in a week. I have also seen bromeliads, lilies, and succulents being sold as orchids. Hold onto your wallet and buy only if you are absolutely sure of what you're getting. And only if the price is good.

BIG-BOX STORES AND CHAIN STORES

For availability and price, big chain stores like Costco, Home Depot, and Safeway are great. Indeed, in many parts of the country, these are the stores that are introducing orchids to the area for the first time. The chains tend to sell orchids that are stronger and easier to grow, and that travel well. This is a good place for beginning orchid owners to start, as you are buying proven orchids at a manageable price point. The downside is that you cannot expect a lot of help at these stores. The employees are not trained orchid experts. Sometimes, information sheets are given with the orchid, or there is a little "how to grow" note with the orchid, which helps. Just be sure to do your homework so you know how to care for the plant you buy. And be sure that the orchid has not suffered too much in its travels (see "What to Look For," page 16).

ORCHID SHOWS

Every major city and many smaller communities around the world hold annual orchid shows. International orchid shows, such as the Pacific Orchid Exposition in San Francisco, the Miami and Redland shows in Florida, and the Tokyo Dome show in Japan, host scores of orchid vendors selling a diversity of orchids and mounting displays that stagger the imagination. Orchid shows can be a bit overwhelming, especially to the first-time buyer, but do not be afraid and go forth. You will be amazed by what you see, and you will be surrounded by people who know all about orchids. You should bring money because you will never see some of these types of orchids again.

Oncidium and intergeneric hybrids give us striking colors and exciting display potential.

TIPS FOR BUYING AT ORCHID SHOWS

GO TO THE PREVIEW
Almost all orchid shows, regardless of size, have a preview or party before the actual show opens. There is usually an extra charge for this, but the price is worth it, as you will get first pick of the plants. Sometimes the best plants are gone before the regular show even starts!

BE SURE TO SEE EVERY VENDOR
Sometimes the smaller, less-flashy vendors have the choice orchids. So be thorough.

GO THE LAST HOURS OF THE LAST DAY
Most vendors do not want to schlep plants back home with them, so the end of a show is a great time to bargain. Just do so politely, and be sure to have cash.

SAMPLE PLANTS

Many vendors will display blooming orchids as samples of the seedlings they are selling. These are usually marked "Sample" or "Not for sale," but sometimes the vendors are willing to sell them. Don't be afraid to ask, especially if the show is coming to an end.

ONLINE AND MAIL ORDER CATALOGS

If you live in a remote area with no access to orchids, online or mail order catalogs may be your only option. It is tricky to ship a blooming orchid, but luckily, orchid shipping and packing has improved. Always request overnight shipping or the fastest shipping process to get your prize home as quickly as possible.

Ordering online or from catalogs is a good option for advanced and serious growers who are looking for specific plants and seedlings not available locally. This is often the only way to obtain some of the rarer species. But buying sight unseen is definitely risky—in general, it is always better to see, touch, and smell the orchid before you purchase. I have bought plants both online and through catalogs and have received some orchids that exceeded my expectations and others that were disappointing.

Buying for Your Lifestyle

If you are a busy person who works long hours, travels a lot, or is away from home most of the week, you should not buy orchids that require daily watering. Only purchase what you can maintain. Here is a list of the more "high-maintenance" orchids:

❖ *Plants in tiny pots* / Orchids in small pots (4 inches wide or less) require daily or frequent

WHERE TO FIND THE BEST BARGAINS

The best bargains on orchids can appear at places you would never dream of finding an orchid. I have bought orchids for great prices at antiques stores, bookstores, food festivals, and county fairs. The other best places for good bargains are:

BIG-BOX AND CHAIN GROCERY STORES
There are great deals to be found here, especially during markdown times. If you are careful about buying a healthy plant, you can find excellent deals.

GARDEN CENTERS AND PLANT NURSERIES / This is where you find the hidden bargains. Sometimes these growers don't even realize that a particular plant is an orchid and sell it for one-fifth the price as the orchid shop across town. I bought my favorite *Laelia canariensis*, which is to this day the best clone I have ever seen, at a cactus store in Southern California for $10.

ESTATE AND GARAGE SALES / I have found more bargains at estate sales than garage sales. Often, the orchids at estate sales are in excellent condition because large estates have gardeners tending their orchids over the years. The orchids at garage sales tend to be in poor condition (usually the owners have given up on the orchids, and that is why they are being sold). But even among the junk, there are treasures to be found. I once found a beautiful and flawless *Angraecum veitchii* that had been grown in someone's house for years in an east-facing window. The foliage was beautifully green, with no damage at all on the leaves. The plant was worth $500, and I got it for $20!

THE DEADLY RIDE HOME

Now that you have carefully selected your orchid, asked the seller all the right questions, and paid the right price, it is time to get that orchid home.

I would estimate that 10 percent of orchids bought by novices never make it home alive, and that another 10 percent suffer significant damage. Orchids will sustain injury if not properly shaded and cooled. The sun is the main culprit: it takes only five to twenty minutes in direct sunlight through a car window for an orchid to become damaged. This can happen even when the windows are open or the air conditioning is on. When orchids get severely burned, the flowers and leaves wither almost instantly. But more often the burn is moderate, and the damage shows up slowly over a few days. Symptoms of moderate burning include unopened flower buds turning yellow and dropping off, leaves spotting or turning yellow and falling off, and—sadly—the general collapse of the entire plant. Here are some tips for getting your precious orchid home safely:

✤ On sunny days, do your shopping early or late in the day and go directly home afterward.

✤ Secure the plant in the car so it can not fall by wedging it in the seat using crumpled newspaper or clothing. You can even buckle larger orchids in with a seatbelt.

✤ Shade the plant and the flowers from the sun, either by placing the plant in the middle of the car away from the windows, or by covering the windows with newspaper.

✤ If you must stop, park in the shade and roll down the windows, just as you would with a pet.

attention. Try to buy orchids in larger pots that can retain more water if you are gone all week. A 5- or 6-inch pot is more realistic.

✤ *Mounted orchids* / Whether grown on tree fern or cork, mounted orchids do not like to left alone for too long. They need daily showers, so it is difficult to keep a mounted orchid thriving if you are gone most of the time (see page 42 for more on mounting orchids).

✤ *Net pots* / Even if this type of pot is 6 inches wide, it can dry out quickly (see page 43 for more on net pots).

✤ *Orchids grown in sphagnum moss* / Sphagnum moss is an unforgiving growing medium. If it dries out even a little, you have to soak it in order to revive the moss and avoid repotting. If the moss dries out completely, the plant will die, making this growing medium a poor choice for people who spend much time away from home (see page 31 for more on growing in sphagnum moss).

Part Two

GROWING ORCHIDS

GETTING TO KNOW YOUR ORCHID

Now that you have purchased the orchid of your dreams and gotten it home safely, the real fun begins.

READ THIS BEFORE YOU CUT!

Just like us, orchids can catch viruses. The most common way this happens is any part of an orchid is cut with scissors that have been inadvertently used to cut a virused plant . Always sterilize your scissors by holding them in an open flame before you cut any part of your orchid!

The first thing to do when you get home is to water the orchid. Bring it to the sink and, using room-temperature water and without getting the flowers wet, fully water the plant and allow it to drain. Then pick up the orchid and examine it closely, really closely. Spend a minute checking out the leaves and bulbs and how they are growing: look underneath the leaves for bugs and try to identify the newest and oldest leaves and bulbs to familiarize yourself with the state of the orchid. Look at the flower spikes and make a mental note of how many flowers and buds there are. Notice how readily the water drains from the pot and note the weight of the plant in your hand after it has been watered.

These observations will be your reference point. You are examining the plant so that when any new growth or damage to the leaves appears, you will notice. You are weighing the plant so that you can learn its weight when it is wet. When the plant is dry and needs watering, it weighs less, so this is an easy way to tell if it needs watering. You should monitor your orchid closely for the first few weeks, checking it and weighing it every three days to determine how long it takes for the orchid to dry out.

You may discover that in your home, you only need to water your orchid once every ten days. Being in tune with the orchid's needs from the beginning will help you care for it over time.

Location, Location, Location

You may already have a location for your orchid in mind: the entryway, the dining room table, a bathroom shelf, the bedside table. Find your location and place your beloved orchid in its new home. But before you leave it there, you must make sure your orchid is safe. There are hidden threats all over any house, and you don't want your orchid to be damaged as soon as you get it home.

DANGEROUS SITUATIONS

Make sure the plant isn't directly next to heating and cooling vents or a very sunny window. These locations will damage your orchid's flowers and the unopened flower buds, and eventually kill the plant due to extreme temperature fluctuations. Other problematic locations include:

* *The mantel* / Orchids look magnificent on a fireplace mantel, but if you start a fire the rising heat will roast your flowers.

* *The kitchen* / A Thanksgiving Day cooking fest can raise the heat in the room and wither orchids blooming in the kitchen. It is fine to keep an orchid in the kitchen, albeit not too close to the stove, but move it to another room while cooking for extended periods of time.

* *Spotlights or high-intensity lights* / These can wither flowers in just one evening, especially when the lights are focused directly on the orchid. (A good alternative is to backlight the orchid instead—see page 112.)

* *Drafty areas* / Cold or warm drafty areas can play havoc with an orchid that is still in the

Be careful not to place your orchids too close to the window—they could get burned by the sun's rays coming through the glass.

process of blooming. The rapidly changing temperatures also make it hard for the orchid to get into a temperature-and-growth rhythm, as natural day and night warm and cool periods are disrupted. Drafty areas of the house usually include entryways and hallways, both popular locations for orchids. If you want to place your orchid in a drafty location, select a plant that has fully bloomed, with no unopened flower buds. Because the flowers are mature, they have hardened and will last longer in an environment that is too drafty for buds to open successfully.

✤ *High-traffic areas* / It's best not to place your orchid in a space where the flowers are constantly being bumped and banged by people walking down the hall or coming into the house. With tall orchids like oncidiums, you also have to be careful that they do not arch over into traffic areas where they can catch in people's hair and become damaged.

✤ *Consider pets* / Orchids on low tables and big dogs with tails do not work well together. Or worse—something that happened to me—a low table and a Labrador who likes to eat orchids. I have seen many beautiful orchid flowers ripped to shreds by bored housecats. Parrots and other birds have been known to pick at orchids and kill them. Remember to protect your plants from your furred and feathered friends.

✤ *Darkness* / If the location for your orchid is a room that has no windows and is very dark, avoid choosing an orchid that has not fully bloomed. Without any light, flower buds will fail to develop. Place only orchids whose flowers are fully opened in these types of locations.

If you are attached to a special location, say on that new table behind the sofa that just happens to be directly above a heating vent, you must make adjustments in order to keep your orchid healthy. Close the heating vent, pull the drapes during the day, and check the conditions often. Otherwise, you will be saying goodbye to your orchid all too soon.

TOO HOT TO HANDLE: BUD BLASTING

Wide temperature fluctuations will injure your orchid. A quick rise or drop in temperature causes a discrepancy between the outside and the inside temperatures of the flower bud, which results in the bud yellowing and dropping. This is called "bud blasting." In nature, orchids grow with gradual temperature fluctuations, so dramatic changes should always be avoided.

CHECKLIST FOR ORCHIDS

AVOID
1. Heating and cooling vents
2. Direct sun
3. Total darkness
4. Hot spotlights and lighting
5. Child- and pet-accessible locations

SEEK OUT
1. Bright light
2. Good air circulation
3. Good humidity
4. A calm environment

When growing on a windowsill, it is very important to note the plant's orientation to the sun and return it to its exact position after watering.

THE BEST ROOM IN THE HOUSE

It is truly amazing how well orchids can adapt to a home's environment. I have seen types of orchids growing in houses that I would have recommended being only inside a controlled greenhouse. Anything is possible. Still, consider the environments of different rooms before parking your orchid somewhere permanently.

✤ KITCHENS
Most kitchens have all the right ingredients for a successful orchid habitat: bright light, good humidity, good air circulation, and easy access to watering. However, the excessive temperature changes can be damaging, so you must be careful.

✤ BATHROOMS
I have had great luck growing orchids in the bathroom. One of the first "rare" orchids I ever bloomed was a species of Bulbophyllum growing on a piece of hanging tree-fern root that I kept in my shower about 2 feet from an east-facing shaded window. I had read that the orchid came from the rain forest, where

it rained every night, so I just left it in the shower, and it bloomed twice a year until I moved and brought it to a "real" greenhouse with ideal conditions—where it promptly died. (Love hurts.) Bathrooms usually have everything you need to make your orchid feel at home: good light, high humidity, warmth, and access to water. However, if your bathroom is dark, with no windows, your orchid will prefer another spot in the house.

✤ WINDOWSILLS
Many orchid growers claim that north- and east-facing windowsills are the best places to grow small orchids indoors. These can be windowsills in living rooms, bedrooms, sunrooms, or anywhere. I have had success

growing on north-facing windowsills, especially with miniature orchids. In my experience, south-, east-, and west-facing sills can present problems, as the sun's position changes throughout the year. In these locations, you will have to monitor your orchids to make sure they do not get too much sunlight. Also, make sure they are not too close to the glass or touching the glass, as the sun's rays will burn the leaves on sunny days. In winter, the cold glass can also hurt the leaves. Condensation on the windows can also run onto the leaves, causing excess moisture and rot.

✤ LAUNDRY ROOMS

If your laundry room has a sink and a window, this could be the mini jungle you have been looking for. There are usually few interior design issues with a laundry room, and you can spread your orchids out. If you do a lot of laundry, the increased humidity and warmth will keep your orchids thriving (and sparkling clean). But again, if there is no natural light, this is not an ideal location to grow your orchids. But you can bring one in for company now and then when you're doing your laundry.

✤ SUNROOMS

If you are lucky enough to live in an older home with a sunroom or conservatory, your orchids will love you. These rooms were designed to grow plants, and have southern, eastern or western exposure. I have been in older homes where the sunrooms have tiled floors with floor drainage and hose outlets, which makes watering a dream. Your orchids will love all the natural sunlight, and if too much sun is a problem, there are many easy fixes for shading, from simple drapes to whitewashing your windows. If you have a sunroom with northern exposure, your high-light orchids such as oncidiums should be grown elsewhere in the house, but your pathiopedilums and phalaenopsis will do well here.

Grow, Baby, Grow
SIX KEY REQUIREMENTS FOR HEALTHY ORCHIDS

The beautiful thing about growing orchids is that there are a zillion different kinds of these plants that will grow in a zillion different ways. Each type of orchid is unique, and each type dictates whether it is best grown in warm, intermediate, or cool temperatures (which is why it is so important to know the type). The potting medium and the size of the pot dictate how often the orchid should be watered.

Remember that your orchid is one of the most evolved plants on earth. No other plant is so widely distributed around the world, or as adaptable and pollinator specific. It will readily adapt to your space, especially if you try to adapt your space to it. Successful home orchid-growing requires that you accommodate, as well as you can, the basic needs of an orchid: light, potting, water, fertilizer, air circulation, and humidity.

LIGHT

Think about the sunniest and brightest locations in your home. Here in the United States, southern exposure is the strongest, so put your vandas and dendrobiums and other light-loving types there. Western exposure (afternoon) is the next strongest, followed by eastern (morning), and the darkest, or lowest exposure, is northern. Remember, the brighter the light, the more watering required.

✤ TRICKS FOR LIGHTING

If you have only low light levels in your house, fear not. I've come across a few tricks over the years that will help you provide optimal lighting for your precious plant.

Use mirrors to increase light / A well-placed mirror placed opposite the window or light source can double the amount of light in a space. By adjusting the angle of the mirror reflecting the light, you can focus on normally darker areas.

Consider using a grow light / This will increase your chances of good growth and flowering. Plant grow lights are available in a variety of styles and shapes. If you are just beginning, I recommend starting with the simple bulb type.

Monitor the plant's orientation to the light source / It is important to notice which side of the plant is facing the light and to keep this consistent. To do this, place a plant label or tag in the pot and make sure the tag is always in the same position. (facing same way). For example, if you place a tag in the front of the pot as you face it, after moving the plant to water or repot, place it back in its spot with the tag in the same position. By being kept in the same orientation to the light, the orchid will not waste energy repeatedly bending toward the light. Also, if the unexposed leaves and foliage are suddenly exposed to direct sunlight, they will often burn. Consistency is key.

Too much of a good thing / If you live in a glass house with direct sun exposure all day long and you want to grow shade-loving orchids such as phalaenopsis, you will need to have drapes for your windows. I recommend sheer drapes or bamboo shades that allow some light to pass through. Horticultural shade cloth, available at nurseries and online, is also a good shading option. The cloth comes in black or white, with different shading levels available. Twenty to forty percent shading is good for the house. You can cut it easily with scissors to fit the inside of the window to be shaded, where it can be attached using tape. It is then easy to move throughout the year as the sun's position changes. White tissue paper can be used in the same way, using multiple layers to increase the amount of shading.

POTTING

Potting and repotting is probably the beginner's biggest challenge. If you want to keep that orchid you just bought for the next twenty years, you will have to repot it many times, so you must not fear the orchid pot.

To begin, you have to know what your orchid is planted in and how long that planting medium retains water. Different potting media have different water-retention abilities. The size and type of pot make a big difference as well, as a small 1- or 2-inch pot can dry out in a day, while a 6-inch pot typically takes a week to dry out. Clay pots dry out faster than plastic ones. A 6-inch pot with large orchid bark dries out faster than a 6-inch pot with fine-size bark.

❖ **WHEN TO REPOT**

Orchids have different growth cycles, so I have included specific guides for the twelve major types of commercial orchids in Part Three. However, there are some general guidelines to follow. Repotting is a key link in good orchid growing, and it is very easy to send an orchid into a downhill spiral by repotting it in the middle or end of its growth cycle. Generally speaking, the best time to repot an orchid is when it is just beginning a new growth cycle, usually after the plant has finished blooming. The beginning of the growth cycle is apparent by new roots and growth in the plant. Look at the base of the plant for new white roots and green tips or at the top of the plant for new growth. Most orchids have a yearly growth cycle, but there are many, especially among the smaller and miniature types that will have two and sometimes three growth periods a year, so do not depend on waiting until after they flower, but examine your plants when you water for new growth.

❖ **WHAT TO USE**

I have seen orchids grown in everything, and I mean everything—marbles, wine corks, socks— you name it. I am all for experimentation, but I personally stick with sphagnum moss, orchid bark, orchid bark mixes, and, more recently, a new redwood fiber that is a wood by-product.

Three popular potting mixes / Left: Fir or redwood shredded bark; Center: Sphagnum Moss; Right: Redwood bark and perlite mix.

Sphagnum Moss / Sphagnum moss is the live moss that grows on top of peat bogs. The dried moss is imported to the States from Chile and New Zealand. I love this stuff and use it a lot. Most orchids thrive when potted in this medium. The roots love the airy moss. Sphagnum moss is available wherever orchids are sold, even in the nursery sections of big-box stores.

The moss is sold either bagged or in a bale. Remove what you think you will need, put it in a tray of water, and let it soak, breaking up the compressed bunches so that the strands of moss are able to absorb the water. Let the moss sit for 10 minutes and then drain to use.

Unfortunately, sphagnum moss is the most unforgiving potting mix there is—meaning that it loses its ability to absorb water after completely drying out. A well-growing orchid potted in sphagnum moss that has dried out completely will have to be repotted; that is, you will have to remove the orchid from the pot, remove and discard the old moss, and repot the orchid in fresh moss. Sphagnum moss is also the most expensive orchid mix on the market; prices can range from $8 to $20 for a 1-pound bag.

Orchid Bark / Orchid bark is the most common orchid potting medium today, available at most plant nurseries and garden centers. Commercial orchid bark comes in three sizes: large, medium,

and small. Usually, the size of the orchid roots determines the size of the orchid bark to be used, but there are some exceptions, so you have to know what type of orchid you have. In general, you use large-size bark with orchids with large roots, like vandas and ryncostylis. Orchids with medium-size roots, such as dendrobiums and cattleyas, call for medium-size bark, and orchids with smaller, skinnier roots such as oncidiums do best in small-size bark. Note that the larger the size of bark used, the quicker the pot dries out. Always wet and rinse the bark before using.

Orchid Bark Mix / While many orchid purists prefer a bark-only mix, I think the addition of medium-size perlite (to help keep the bark airy and prevent compression) and charcoal (to improve aeration in the mix and absorb excess fertilizer) helps orchid roots maintain growth and adds to the longevity of the mix in general. To make this mix, combine one-half part garden charcoal pieces (available at nurseries and plant shops) to one part medium- or large-size perlite to two parts orchid bark. Mix, soak for an hour, and rinse and drain before potting.

Redwood Fiber / Shredded redwood bark, also called "gorilla hair," is a new orchid-growing medium readily available at orchid supply stores and some larger chains. Sold in one- to three-cubic-foot bags, it is the least expensive of all the potting mediums. When you take it out of the bag, you will notice it is a little "dirty," with pieces of wood and branches of varying size mixed in. Remove all wood and solid debris and pull the fibers that are still compressed apart. Then take what you need, soak it for a few minutes in water to improve the fiber flexibility, and drain. I have seen a diverse selection of orchids grown in this medium and have been very impressed with the root growth.

❖ **POTS: CLAY VS. PLASTIC**
Many growers swear by the unglazed clay pots made exclusively for orchids, with drainage

holes added on the bottom and sides that allow for perfect drainage and air exposure. The classic standard for orchid growing, these pots are available at nurseries, orchid supply stores, and wherever tropical plants are sold. Both sphagnum moss and orchid bark mixes can be used with clay with success. A well-draining clay pot coupled with sphagnum moss is a great combination for a multitude of orchid types, and is my preferred recipe for success.

These clay orchid pots are preferable to regular unglazed clay pots with a single drainage hole, which can prevent good drainage. But all clay pots will dry out quicker than plastic pots. Also, orchid roots strongly adhere to clay, which can be a problem when it comes time for repotting. Bark mixes, sphagnum moss, and redwood fiber all work well with clay pots, but both sphagnum and redwood fiber dry out much quicker in clay pots than in plastic pots. Clay pots are also more expensive than plastic pots.

Glazed ceramic orchid pots are also used, and while more attractive, have lost the desirable porous attributes of the natural clay, and do not "breathe," keeping the roots and potting mix wetter longer, making it easier to overwater and rotting the roots. If using glazed pottery,

choose pots with multiple drainage holes to ensure good drainage and air exposure.

Almost all orchids sold in the marketplace are planted in plastic pots now custommade for orchid growing, with increased drainage holes at the bottom and bottom sides of the pot. Some plastic pots have a raised cone at the bottom of the pot, which greatly increases air flow and water drainage. You can use orchid bark, sphagnum moss, or redwood fiber when potting in plastic. The downside to plastic pots is that they are unattractive and need to be placed inside cachepots or other decorative containers.

✤ HOW TO REPOT

First, slowly and carefully remove the plant from its pot by grasping the base of the plant and tugging on it. You will probably want to work over a tray or a potting table to keep from making too much of a mess. If the plant is growing

A typical commercial phalaenopsis in need of repotting.

Modern plastic orchid pots. Note the abundance of drainage holes and raised rims and corners to ensure good drainage. Upper right hand corner: a "net" pot.

Cool-growing oncidiums and masdevallias growing outside in San Francisco, with shade protection.

in a plastic pot and refuses to budge, first look underneath the pot and to see if any roots have grown through the drainage holes and are attached to the pot. If this is the case, cut them away. If the pot is square, you can squeeze the opposite corners to loosen the mix and release the root ball. If it is a round pot, squeeze in the opposite sides while going around the pot and slowly lifting the plant out.

For orchids stuck in clay pots, wet the pot, take a dull dinner knife, and insert it between the root mass and the pot. Slowly work the knife around the inside of the pot with a sawing motion, lifting the orchid as you go, until the roots are free.

Once the plant is out of the pot, look at the roots and root system closely and determine which of the three main types of planting medium the orchid had been growing in. If the plant looks healthy, stick with the same type of medium. If the plant is growing in a medium-size bark mix in a plastic pot, replicate that combination. If it is growing well in moss in a clay pot, replicate that.

❖ WHAT SIZE POT SHOULD I USE?

If the orchid has a bulb or bulbs and a lot of good roots, look at the size of the bulbs and select a pot that is big enough to allow for two new bulbs, or two years of growth. If the root system is poor, with few roots, use a pot that has room for only one new bulb. If the plant has no bulbs and a lot of good roots, pick a pot that is at least 2 inches larger than the previous one, which should allow for two years of growth. Cut off any part of the rhizome or stem that is dead and has no roots.

❖ REPOTTING IN ORCHID BARK

When using orchid bark or an orchid bark mix, shake and gently wash away as much of the old bark as you can. If some roots are clinging to pieces of bark and the bark appears clean, just leave them on. Trim away any dead

Repotting a phalaenopsis using medium-size redwood bark. Note how the base of the plant is held level with the top of the pot while the pot is filled.

Repotting. Note how the mix is being added evenly on all sides of the pot.

roots by cutting them off as close to the bulbs or rhyzome as possible. Look at the plant and find the base of the plant, which is the top of the root-ball, where the new growth occurs. The base should be at the top level of the bark or mix in the new pot; the base should be exposed, not covered. Holding the plant suspended in the pot at the right level, gently pour in the bark or mix, rotating the pot as you fill it up. Push and tap the bark or mix in so the plant is very secure. If the plant is wobbly or top heavy, insert a stake, cut at an angle, into the bark or mix and fasten it securely to the stem using garden wire, floral wire, raffia, or orchid clips, so that the plant will not shift.

NO ROOTS AT ALL?
MAKE YOUR OWN BIONIC ROOTS!

It is not unusual for an orchid to lose all its roots, and although this slows them down, the orchid is still viable and alive. (Sometimes orchids are even imported and sold this way.) To best secure a rootless plant in a pot, make replacement "roots" out of wire. To do this, take a length of wire twice the depth of the pot, fold it over the bulb or rhizome, and twist twice to firmly attach it. Then take the two lengths of wire hanging down and coil them around your finger to make two coils to place in the pot in lieu of roots. Pot normally, and the wires will serve as "roots" to help secure and hold the orchid in the pot. You can also use a stake to provide extra support. The more steadfast the orchid is in the pot, the quicker new (real) roots will appear.

Repotting with sphagnum moss. Note how the moist moss is "woven" into the existing roots.

Now, set the plant in the sink or a bathtub and water the planting medium gently to rinse out any loose material and make sure the pot is draining well and the drainage holes are not plugged with bark or mix.

✤ REPOTTING WITH SPHAGNUM MOSS

If the plant is already growing in moss and has a nice solid root-ball, use prepared wet moss

(see page 31) and a pot that will allow for two years' new growth. Lay a bed of moss in the bottom of the pot to elevate the orchid so that the base is not buried, then fill in the sides of the pot, gently pushing down the moss until the plant is secure in the pot. When adding a flower stake for support, use a pencil sharpener to sharpen the end to be inserted into the moss rather than just cutting the stake at an angle, as moss is easily compressed and a sharply pointed stake will instead displace the moss, keeping the stake more secure. Fasten the stake to the orchid with garden wire, floral wire, raffia, or orchid clips, *then* water the plant. The moss will swell slightly when watered, so make sure the top of the moss stays under the rim of the pot by at least ½ inch. This allows water to puddle in the pot, as moss is slower to absorb water than bark. If your orchid has few roots, make a little ball of moss and wrap the roots around it. Repot in a smaller pot, and lay moss in from the sides until secure. Water, then check the drainage.

❖ REPOTTING WITH REDWOOD FIBER

Using the prepared clean and wet fiber (see page 31), work the fiber between the roots of the orchid and wedge it in from all sides of the pot. You might want to cut up the fiber if the pieces are too long or condensed. The fiber packs up quickly and you don't want it to be too tight, so add new pieces slowly. Water when done and make sure all the drainage holes are clear.

Repotting using redwood fiber. Be sure to weave the fiber between the roots. Take your time.

WATERING

Orchids are just like us: they need water to live. The key to growing a successful plant is to know how often it needs water. This depends on the size of the pot and the medium the orchid is planted in. Modern improvements in orchid hardiness and in potting media have lengthened the amount of time between necessary waterings.

Watering weekly is the general rule for an orchid in a 6-inch plastic pot, but this is not true if you are experiencing a heat wave and the orchid is drying out completely in two days, or if it has been raining for three weeks and humidity is high and the orchid is still wet and the pot is heavy ten days after the last watering. You must pick up the pot to check. Watering for an orchid's unique needs will result in a healthy plant. A healthy plant will result in flowers.

Water drainage is very important, as it is difficult to overwater an orchid when the drainage is good. If your orchid is not draining, clear the drainage holes of debris and check again.

One thing that is a little tricky is that the symptoms of both overwatering and underwatering can be similar. When the orchid is under-watered, the roots will dry and collapse, leading to shriveled buds and leaves that turn brown and drop. When the plant is overwatered, the root system can rot and collapse, and the bulbs will shrivel and the leaves drop. But in either case, the plant and the pot will be either dry and needing water, or too wet, and you should reduce the watering schedule. If the plant has lost its root system, which will make it loose in the pot, remove the plant from the pot. Then remove all the dead roots and and repot as recommended (see page 35). An orchid can lose all its roots, survive, grow all new roots, and still bloom on schedule.

❖ HOW TO WATER

To give your orchid a good watering, bring it to a deep sink, shower, or tub—any area big enough where you can water the entire plant. Make sure the water is at room temperature. Use a spray head if possible, making sure the water pressure is not so high that it knocks the potting media out of the pot. Profusely water the orchid bulbs, the top and bottom of the leaves, and the pot, checking the bottom of the pot to make sure the pot is draining. I do not generally water the flowers, as this can cause spotting on some orchids if there is not adequate air circulation for it to evaporate quickly. Regularly rinsing the plant in this way keeps pests like mites away and makes your orchid happy.

So you're going away and worried about your new orchid. What to do?

FOR ONE TO TWO DAYS / Make sure you water before you go, and check the orchid first thing when you get back.

FOR THREE TO FIFTEEN DAYS / Place the plant in a sink or bathtub with good light; these are great vacation houses for orchids. Set the plant on an inverted cup or bowl to elevate it, close the drain, and fill the sink or tub to just below the bottom of the orchid pot, making a little pool to create humidity and help keep the plant wet longer.

FOR FIFTEEN TO THIRTY DAYS / Place the plant in a bathtub or sink as above, and have a friend come by to water weekly, draining and refilling the bathtub or sink, being sure the water level stays below the bottom of the orchid pots.

After a thorough watering, allow the plant to drain for a few minutes. If your air circulation is poor, make sure no water has collected on the leaves or in the crown, where the new leaves are emerging out of the orchid, as this can rot new growth or create black rot spots on the leaves. Tilting your orchid on its side and allowing the water to drain out, or blowing into the crown to drive the water out are good after-watering habits to avoid water collecting on or in the orchids. If there is still water on the orchid, wipe the orchid off with a soft cotton cloth.

It's true that watering a display orchid can be a hassle, as you must first move the orchid to where you are watering, then remove any moss used for topping and remove the orchid from its cachepot before watering. Then you must allow time for the water to drain after watering, and finally you have to replace everything. But it's worth it to go to the trouble (especially if you water just once a week), as this is by far the best way to keep your orchid hydrated and healthy.

WATERING ORCHIDS IN PLASTIC POTS PLANTED WITH SPHAGNUM MOSS

It is important to know that when orchids are planted with sphagnum moss in plastic pots, the moss dries out from the bottom up! This is odd but true, and the old orchid myth of never watering an orchid when it is wet can get you in trouble here, as the top of the pot can be wet, but the bottom dry. Do not let this fool you, and always check the weight of the pot to be sure it is heavy with water.

❖ MISTING

Unless you are growing mounted small hanging orchids (see page 42), I do not recommend misting as your primary watering mode as misters do not deliver enough water to drench a plant. Using a hand mister periodically does supplement the relative humidity, and the orchids love the extra water. But misting should only be done in the early morning or late in the day and never when there is sunlight on the leaves, because tiny water drops can act as a magnifying lens for sun rays and burn and spot your orchid. And be sure to blow or shake any excess water off the flowers after misting.

❖ WATERING TRICKS

Do not water your plants with water you wouldn't drink yourself. If your water quality is poor, consider a purification system for both you and your orchids. I was at a home once where they had a beautiful purification system for their orchids, but used water that smelled like burnt matches straight from the tap for themselves. I drank the orchid water.

Never use cold or hot water to water your orchids. Orchid cells close when cold, thus the roots do not efficiently absorb cold water, and hot water damages them. Keep the water at room temperature; that is, tepid, or lukewarm.

FERTILIZING

For some reason, fertilizing is a hard first step for some beginners to take. The process is an easy one if you just follow directions on the orchid fertilizer you purchase, so do not be shy. Your orchid is waiting, and it is hungry.

There are many different opinions among orchid growers about how often and what to use to fertilize orchids. Over the years I tried many different ways of fertilizing my orchids: with every watering, once a week, once every two weeks, or once a month, and with all kinds of different fertilizers. The most important thing I have learned is that for an orchid to grow well it must be fed.

❖ **WHAT TYPE OF FERTILIZER SHOULD I USE?**
Orchid fertilizers come in three forms: 1/ liquid, which is usually concentrated and has to be diluted; 2/ powder, which is dissolved in water; and 3/ granular. The last type is a slow-release fertilizer that is sprinkled on the base of the plant to release nutrients each time the plant is watered.

A Burrageara Nellie Isler growing in a hanging pot.

DORMANCY IN ORCHIDS

Dormancy is a "rest period" when orchids are not growing or blooming. In nature, this period generally occurs in the winter when temperatures drop. Tropical orchids from an area that has a mild seasonal temperature change, or a dry and rainy season, will also have some sort of dormant period. However, dormancy can be tough to pinpoint for household plants. For tropical orchids grown in the house, dormancy can be brought on by changing seasons with less light and heat, which slows the orchid's growth. For orchids like phals and vandas, which are constantly growing, there should not be a dormancy period, yet when grown in the home, these orchids may slow or stop actively growing until favorable conditions return. Reduce watering and fertilizing during dormancy, as the roots are not absorbing as much water or nutrients.

Many different types of orchid and plant fertilizers are available. I prefer organic fertilizers, ideally those that contain trace elements, meaning elements that are present in a natural environment. I've learned that having trace elements in your fertilizer is the key to growing healthy plants, so when choosing, check the label to see if trace elements are included. The three numbers you see on the label of all fertilizers represent the proportion of nitrogen, phosphorus, and potassium in the mix. There are two types of orchid fertilizer: one for growing and one for blooming. Fertilizers for growing contain nitrogen and will have a first number equal to or greater than the last two, such as 12-10-10. Fertilizers for blooming contain no nitrogen, only phosphorus and potassium to promote blooming and flower growth. Blooming fertilizers will have a zero as their first number, for example, 0-10-10. Blooming fertilizers are applied after the bulb and growth have matured and throughout the flowering phase. Once the plant finishes flowering, new growth will begin to appear, and the plant should be given a growing fertilizer instead.

❖ HOW OFTEN SHOULD I FERTILIZE?

There is some variation in frequency of feeding among different types of orchids, but realistically, fertilizing twice a month should be enough. If you choose to use a granular fertilizer, every six months is sufficient.

GRANULAR FERTILIZER

If you know in your heart that there will be times when your orchid will be lucky to get watered, much less fertilized, consider this fertilizer. It takes minutes to use, and you only have to apply it once or twice a year. Just follow the instructions, which typically call for scattering a teaspoon or so of the grains of dry fertilizer on top of the potting medium in the pot and mixing it in lightly. Now, every time you water the granules will slowly release nutrients. This is a good way to insure that your plant is fed but not overfed.

❖ OVERFERTILIZING

If you have never fertilized your orchid, once you begin you will see a big difference after a month or two. You will likely then be tempted to give it more and more and more, but resist this urge.

If you are giving your orchid too much fertilizer you will first see a white residue on the leaves. This is the excess fertilizer and salts. To correct, flush your orchid with water and stop fertilizing for a month. When you begin again, reduce the amount of fertilizer you're using.

You might also notice that the normally green tips of the orchid's new roots emerging from the base of the plant are browned and dead looking. Or, if the plant has aerial roots, the normally green root tips may be brown and the white roots withered or browning in the furrows. This means that the excess salts have burned them. If the roots are burned significantly, your plant will become loose in the pot and should be repotted.

AIR CIRCULATION

The importance of air circulation is underestimated when it comes to orchid culture. Orchids love fresh air and respond to good air circulation. Good air movement fights bud blast by insuring a gradual change of temperature. It also fights leaf and foliage burn by cooling the plant. I am often asked why orchids can be seen growing in direct sun in the wild. This is because in nature, the wind and breezes cool the plant, but in a house that kind of air movement is hard to achieve. Fresh air is good for both you and your orchid, so open those windows.

❖ I recommend opening windows not normally opened, as it is amazing what a difference a simple adjustment like that can make in your overall air circulation.

❖ You might need a fan to improve your air circulation, especially if your growing area gets hot during parts of the day. There are fans of every size and price. We can expect to see more efficient solar fans in our future, which is great. Generally, the bigger the room the bigger the fan you should use. I prefer to use oscillating fans, as they move the air more efficiently than single-directional fans. The fan should be kept a few feet away from your orchids, as you do not want them to be in such a draft that they dry out too quickly. A good test to do is to cut a piece of ribbon and hold it over the plants that are receiving the air. You want the ribbon to lightly flutter. If the ribbon looks like a flag in a windstorm, move the fan farther away. You can put the fan on a timer, or preferably, leave it on all the time.

HUMIDITY

Orchids love humidity. Almost all orchids come from humid environments, and although modern hybrids are bred for dryer conditions, they will grow more quickly and be stronger with good humidity. There are several ways to create humidity:

❖ Pots on top of raised water sources allow water to evaporate underneath the plants without the drainage being affected. I suggest using a sided baking sheet (jelly roll pan) for multiple plants or an old-fashioned metal ice-cube tray for a single plant or several miniature orchids. Place same-size pebbles in the pan (you can find these in bags in garden stores) and add water to the pan to just below the top of the pebbles. Place the pot on top of the pebbles. Plastic plant saucers work as well, the larger the better; always use a saucer at least twice the size of the pot to hold as much water as possible.

❖ If you live in a very dry house in an arid climate, mini humidifiers can also do the trick, especially if you grow a large number of orchids. These are available at big-box stores.

❖ Another way to revive an orchid that looks dehydrated, that is, appears shriveled and dry, is to make a little "greenhouse" for it. This is not practical for orchids that are on display, of course, but if you have an orchid rehabilitation spot, place it on a waterproof tray filled with pebbles, add water to just below the top of the pebbles, and attach a clear plastic bag over the orchid, pot, and tray, tucking the bag under the tray to create a space where the humidity is contained. The main problem with this setup is that there is

Phalaenopsis hybrids growing under shaded "Whitewashed" glass.

no air circulation inside the plastic bag, and the lack of circulation and the increased condensation allows excess water to collect on the plant, which can cause rot. So be careful to monitor your orchid, and remove the plastic bag as soon as the orchid begins to look plump and healthy again. Note: Do not place your "greenhouse" in direct sunlight, as this can heat up the interior of the plastic bag and kill the orchid in one day.

Oncidium mounted on tree fern. Note how the wire wrapping is over the rhizome and not in the way of emerging growth.

Mounting Orchids

If you are lucky enough to see an orchid blooming in the jungle, it will usually be growing on a tree, either on the trunk or in the branches. An orchid naturally growing in the air on a branch or trunk is a beautiful thing, as the roots tightly grasp the host and run along the branches. Mounting an orchid on a piece of wood, cork, or tree fern provides a natural environment for the plant and a bit of visual interest for your home, so don't be afraid to try it.

MOUNTING MEDIA

There are several options for mounting orchids these days. Growers are always discussing what kind of medium is best to use for mounting, but I think it all depends on your home and your watering habits.

❖ **TREE FERN SLABS**
These cut pieces of tree fern "trunk," which are actually compacted dried roots, are easy to find in garden centers. You can buy them in a variety of sizes, thicknesses, and densities, with or without wire hooks attached. Tree fern slabs drain water quickly and retain very little moisture (the thicker the density of the slab, the better the water retention). In the house, orchids planted on tree fern require more watering than do orchids in pots, so grow

these in your kitchen and/or bathroom, where there is easy access to water and drainage. The species of tree ferns used for this product were once overharvested, causing ecological damage, but are now being grown for the marketplace.

❖ **CORK SLABS**
Cork slabs are a renewable resource, which makes them an attractive option for many people. Cork slabs are made of the bark of cork trees, which grows back after being stripped from the trunks. Use the outside, or corky side, to mount the orchid. You can buy the slabs in almost any size you want, from 4 inches to 4 feet long. Orchid roots attach well to cork, firmly gripping the slab. However, as with orchids grown on tree fern, orchids grown on cork slabs will dry out quickly, so they should also be grown near good watering

Oncidium mounted on a piece of cork bark. Note how the base is nestled in a natural indentation of the cork, aiding in water retention.

access. In rare situations, when overwatered the cork can become slimy and moldy. When this occurs, cut down on the watering, let the slimy green stuff dry up, and then shave or cut it off to reveal the fresh cork underneath.

✤ BRANCHES AND TREE TRUNKS

This is a great way to grow orchids if you have a space where they can receive daily watering. Generally, most orchids prefer hardwoods, but are adaptable to other woods as well. If the roots refuse to attach themselves to the wood you are using, try another type.

✤ HANGING WOOD-SLAT BASKETS AND NET POTS

With open sides and bottoms, slat baskets (sold with the hangers attached) and net pots (which are made of plastic mesh) require the same frequent watering schedule as do mounted orchids and should be treated as such. Both kinds of containers can be found anywhere orchid supplies are sold, and they are offered in most nursery catalogs. The only drawback to these containers is that the increased drainage and air exposure, while beneficial to the plant, also causes it to drain and dry more quickly. Because of the frequent waterings required, it is best to hang these pots either over a sink or tub, or in a location where they are easily removed for watering.

Another problem with slat and net containers is that it is very difficult to repot to another type of container, because the wooden slats or netting quickly become hopelessly intertwined with the roots, and to remove them you have to rip apart the whole root system. In this case, I recommend just washing and cleaning out all of the old potting mix and putting the container in a larger container of the same type.

WHEN AND HOW TO MOUNT ORCHIDS

The best time to mount your orchid is after it has flowered and new roots are appearing at the base of the plant. The new roots will quickly attach themselves to the new mount. Always position the plant so the newly emerging roots are facing the mount.

If you are moving your orchid from a pot to a slab or branch, wet the orchid and remove it from the pot, then rinse the roots with water until they are free from all potting debris. Hold the slab or branch with one hand and decide where you are going to place the orchid.

If you are using a tree fern slab, mounting is pretty straightforward. You'll need to create a slight indent where you'd like to secure your plant. To do this, use scissors to cut a line about ¼ inch deep horizontally across the middle of the slab. Then cut down on an angle from the top of the slab, clearing out a bit of tree fern and leaving a small space big enough so that it will fit the base of the orchid and the roots that you wish to place there. Holding the orchid in place, use floral wire or raffia to tie the orchid securely to the tree fern so it does not wobble, then water it to make sure it is attached well enough that it will not be dislodged by the force of the water.

If you are using a cork slab, it will probably be slightly curved and the cork will be pitted with natural indentations. Use these curves and indentations to your advantage when positioning your orchid and its roots so that they lie in the crevices and curves where water will collect. Positioning the base and roots in one of these indentations provides a little extra space for the roots to connect with the slab. If your piece of cork is smooth and there are no natural indentations, you can cut into the cork with a knife to create a little nest-shaped area that will fit the base of the orchid. Once you have nestled the orchid into place, use floral wire or raffia to tie the plant and its roots to the cork.

If you are mounting the orchid on a branch, add a bit of sphagnum moss to the spot where you want the orchid to attach. You need only a strand or two. Place the new roots of the orchid onto the attachment site of the branch, usually a fork in the branch. Raffia is best for this, as it will not cut the roots of the plant, but if it's not available, you can use wire, string, or fishing line. Wrap the raffia or other fastening material several times around the base of the orchid and its roots and make sure that the orchid is completely secure. Then water the plant well to make sure the attachment is holding.

Bugs and Pests

When dealing with bugs and pests, never use poisons. It embarrasses me when people in my field recommend using poisons on orchids in the home. There are safe natural alternative methods and treatments available that will not harm you and your loved ones. This section lists some of the most common types of pests and the best natural ways to deal with them.

But first, remember to always clean your plant when dealing with pests. You don't want dead leaves, dead sheaths, or old flowers or flower spikes hiding and protecting more bugs. Remove all old and dying leaves and foliage from the plant. Be careful, as it is easy to break bulbs and new growth when removing old sheaths and leaves by hand. The best way to do this is to first split the leaf or sheath into many strips and remove the strips slowly, one by one, so you won't damage any new growth hidden under the sheaths.

MEALY BUGS

Mealy bugs are little maggots with white hairy tufts. When populations grow, it can almost look as if you have cotton growing on your orchids. This bothersome bug is a common orchid pest, and is one of the easiest to eliminate.

Clean the plant as recommended above. You will likely need to tip the plant and turn it upside down when spraying, so it is a good idea to cover the tops of the pots with plastic wrap so the potting medium doesn't fall out.

Mix warm water with a few drops of liquid soap in a spray bottle. I use organic dishwashing soap, but common liquid dishwashing soap is okay too. If the bug infestation is major, add one part rubbing alcohol to four parts warm water. Spray the plant in a sink, bathtub, shower, or outside. Be thorough, spraying the tops and bottoms of the leaves and covering the entire plant. You must also spray any other plants that were near the infected plant.

Mealy bugs—easy to get rid of, but good hiders.

APHIDS

These look like little skinny green flies with small eyes. This persistent little pest is usually detected by the sticky sap it produces, which accumulates on the leaves and plants under the flowers.

The easiest and safest remedy for aphids is ladybugs. If you have some in your garden, scoop them into a jar and transfer them to your orchid. After they have eaten everything they will fly away looking for new food, so leave the window open, or place the orchid outside during this process. If there are no ladybugs to be found (you can buy them, but they come in bulk), rinsing or spraying the plant with lukewarm water will take care of the problem. The trick is frequent repeated treatments: Rinse again the day after the first treatment and continue to check the plant twice a week for two weeks, rinsing any remaining bugs away.

Aphids. Ladybugs love to eat them.

SCALE

Two major types of scale can be found on orchids. The first, commonly known as hard scale, looks like little, brown, hard, half-dome bumps on the plant. These vary in size and color, and can be found both on top of and underneath the leaves, and in the leaf and bulb crevices. Hard scale causes the leaf or bulb to turn yellow. The second

Hard scale

you notice this yellowing, you have to deal with the scale. Otherwise your foliage will be ruined.

The second type of scale, known as boisduval scale, looks like small, flat, white bumps; bad infestations can look like white patches or colonies. Like hard scale, this scale turns the leaf or bulb yellow. Boisduval scale is my worst enemy. I have seen growers who had been clean and green for years go over to the dark side and use poisons when confronted with boisduval scale.

I treat hard scale by enlisting the entire arsenal of pest-fighting tools: a sprayer filled with two-thirds rubbing alcohol, one-third water, and 10 drops of dishwashing liquid, a cloth, a sponge, an old toothbrush, and Q-tips. I start by wiping the entire plant with the cloth, then sponge the entire plant with the alcohol mixture. Next, I peel back any old leaves or sheaths that haven't been cleaned. Using the toothbrush, I scrub all the areas of the plant where the scale is concentrated and wipe the hard-to-reach areas with Q-tips. I use the sprayer to clean areas where the Q-tips and toothbrush can't reach. I then spray the entire plant again with the same mixture. I repeat this process for three days and keep a close eye on the plant after that.

I treat boisduval scale with the same mixture, but spray the plant first, then clean it with the toothbrush, wipe it with the sponge, and then spray the plant again, making sure there is no scale hiding in crevices of the plant. The process must be repeated in ten days, as boisduval scale is particularly tough to get rid of.

SPIDER MITES

If you see tiny spiders and/or some small webs, you'll know you have spider mites. However, some spider mites are so small that even when using a hand lens all you will see is the slightest bit of webbing. But you will know they are there due to the yellowing of the leaves and the presence of red splotches that are the result of the mite damage. In bad infestations, the underside of the leaves will also be sticky from the mites. Spider mites are the bane of many an indoor orchid grower's existence. Mites thrive and multiply quickly in environments of low humidity and poor air circulation.

Unfortunately, spraying and treating mites is just a temporary solution. If your orchids live in an environment that supports mites, you will always have mites. For a permanent solution, you must try to raise the humidity and increase the air circulation around your plants.

Another option is to buy predatory spider mites, which feed on plant-damaging mites, from your local nursery. You might have to include some of your orchid-growing friends in this venture, as you unfortunately must buy a lot of predatory spider mites at once in most retail stores. However, predatory mites do work. Most are easy to see, and they will hang around on your plants for a while, killing the harmful spider mites and then go elsewhere looking for more.

To avoid mites altogether, make a point of watering the foliage often, especially during hot and dry weather. High humidity will kill most mites.

ROT

It is common for the base of a leaf to rot, causing the leaf to fall off. This usually happens because some water drained into the base of the leaf and there was not sufficient air circulation for the water to evaporate, so it fermented. When this happens, peel off any damaged or rotting leaf sheath and spray the spot with a little rubbing alcohol. With future watering and misting, be sure that the water does not collect in the leaf sheaths or the crown of new growths. If you find some water has collected, tip the plant over so the excess water drains out.

Rot on phalaenopsis. Always cut damaged areas away, so you can see any new damage that occurs.

There is also a kind of rot that affects the roots and spreads into the bulbs and plants. This type of rot is very hard to stop, though it is easy to spot, as the bulbs and/or leaves turn brown and mushy. If you think your orchid might have this kind of rot, remove the plant from the pot and remove all the potting material and the dead roots. Examine the bulb and the stem of the plant. The bulb should be green. If the bulb

Spider mites (magnified)

or stem is black or discolored at all, you must cut all the damaged parts off, down to where only green and healthy growth remains. This kind of rot is a common problem with orchids and is easy to treat, but you must be diligent in examining your plants on a regular schedule so you can nip the problem in the bud. Spray the remaining plant with rubbing alcohol and allow it to dry in a place with good air circulation. Spray again in a couple of hours and then repot in an appropriate pot.

BACTERIA

Harmful plant bacteria (one common type is known as Erwinia) can invade weak or damaged cells and cause leaf spotting or patching. Bacteria can spread fairly quickly on a plant, revealing itself as black spots or patches. You must respond to this threat as soon as you see it. If the spots or patches appear wet or shiny, the bacteria is still alive and will continue to spread; if the patches are dry, the bacteria is dead. To clean off live bacteria, use scissors sterilized with rubbing alcohol and cut off all the damaged parts of the leaves and plants so you can better monitor any new damage. Check back every day for a couple of weeks to make sure you got it all and that there is no new spotting.

How Does Your Orchid Grow?
SYMPODIAL AND MONOPODIAL ORCHIDS

It's important to know how your particular orchid grows, so that you can properly check on its well-being every year or so. The most important thing to know is that all orchids are either sympodial growers or monopodial growers.

SYMPODIAL GROWERS

Sympodial, or multistemmed orchids, grow by producing one or more new bulbs or growths at the plant's base each year (though technically

Sympodial growers produce new growths at the base of the plant.

they are really pseudobulbs that grow from a rhizome). In some orchids, like cattleyas, the bulbs are very prominent, and in leafy orchids like paphiopedilums they join the rhizome and they are not visible at all. The bulbs and rhizomes of these orchids store water and nutrients to help the orchids survive dry seasons. While some sympodial orchids flower only once a year, many types, especially among the miniature orchids, can bloom up to three times a year, and some sympodial species flower year-round; see Oncidium (page 75), Cattleya (page 65), and Cymbidium (page 89).

MONOPODIAL GROWERS

Monopodial, or single-stemmed, growers have no bulbs. Instead, they grow continually in one direction on a stem, with new growth coming from the apex, or end, of the stem rather than from a bulb. The roots and flower spikes emerge from the sides of the stem, and as the orchid grows older and taller, the bottom of the stem will naturally die off; see Phalaenopsis (page 60) and Vanda (page 82). When watering monopodial orchids it is important to realize that the newest roots are those highest on the stem; take care to give these new roots water.

CARE: SYMPODIAL VS. MONOPODIAL

To assess the health of your orchid over time, first determine if it is sympodial or monopodial (look what you've learned already: two good Scrabble words!). If sympodial, find the bulb that last flowered and then look at the new bulb and growth. If the new bulb and leaves are smaller than the old bulb, this shows that the orchid is not doing as well as it did last year. If the new bulb and leaves are the same size as the old bulb and leaves, this means that it is growing well, and the plant should bloom again. If the new bulb and leaves are

Phalaenopsis are the world's most popular monopodial orchid.

larger than the old bulb and leaves, the orchid is doing really well and you can expect a better flowering this year than the year before.

If your orchid is monopodial, look at the newest leaves. The new leaves should be just as large as the old leaves. If the new leaves are mature but smaller and shorter, the plant is not doing as well. If they are the same size or, better yet, larger, the plant is thriving.

All-Natural Tips for Orchid Care

In my years as an orchid enthusiast, I've discovered many natural tips and smart ways to reuse materials that can help your orchid thrive. As you care for your orchid, consider these earth-friendly options.

SINGING IN THE RAIN

All orchids love rainwater. If it is lightly raining and the temperature is in the sixties, put your orchids outside for a couple of hours. You can also collect rainwater and use it to water your orchids. Just make sure you use the water in a few months and that your rainwater collector is always covered, to avoid becoming a breeding ground for mosquitoes.

GRAY WATER

Gray water is wastewater from your bathtub, sinks, or shower. If you are using organic soaps, you can recycle this water. Many people use a combination of gray water and rainwater to water and fertilize their orchids, and this seems to work well.

RECYCLED WATER

Unless their drainage holes are blocked, orchids drain immediately when watered. This is due to the type of materials used for the potting media. To conserve water, place a pan under the pot while watering; the water will collect in the pan and you can reuse it to continue with your watering or use it in a plant tray to increase humidity.

FERTILIZER

The Native Americans showed the pilgrims how to add a fish to the soil when planting corn. Why not take a cue from that and throw a little of that ahi tuna from last Friday night in your orchid pot? Just chop it small and sprinkle it in the pot, or put some leftover fish in the bottom of a pot when repotting. Or, you can use a machine or a mortar and pestle to mash up leftover fish to make a liquid fertilizer. It's true that fish products and seaweed products do smell fishy. That's why using them is more common with outdoor plants.

PEST REPELLENTS

Some of my purist natural friends disdain my use of rubbing alcohol to get rid of pests. I admit I roll my eyes at this a bit because it does work. A good natural alternative is organic liquid soap, which you can find at any natural foods store (use 1 tablespoon per 16-ounce spray bottle). Natural ingredients like garlic and pepper also work as organic pesticides and are safe to use in the house.

POTS

Plastic pots should be used again after being washed thoroughly. You can easily make your own custom-size plastic pots out of old recycled plastic cups, and containers using a sharp knife. Old plastic gallon milk jugs when cut to about 3 inches high with drainage holes added make great pots for orchids that spread and need wide pots that are expensive and hard to find.

Clay pots can also be washed and reused: Using a bucket deep enough to completely submerge the pot, add the juice of two lemons and one lime to every gallon of water. Completely submerge the dirty pot in the bucket and soak for two days, stirring occasionally. Remove the

A NATURAL PESTICIDE FROM THE KITCHEN

1 head garlic
1 teaspoon cayenne pepper
1 tablespoon olive oil
1 tablespoon organic dishwashing liquid
2 cups water

Break the head of garlic into cloves and peel them. In a blender, combine the garlic with the cayenne, oil, soap, and about ½ cup of the water. Blend until the garlic is completely liquefied and puréed. Mix well with the remaining water and apply with a household sprayer. The garlic smell will dissipate quickly; the only negative effect is that your appetite may increase during the procedure.

pot and place it right side up in the sun. Leave out to dry for three days. Reuse water for cleaning.

BARK

You can recycle found wood to make your own bark. Several types of fir trees are used to make orchid bark, and many, including redwood trees, drop their bark naturally. To reuse found bark, clean it first by cutting it up into your desired bark size and steaming it over simmering water in a large covered steamer pot for 30 minutes. After steaming, allow the bark to cool for a day, keeping it isolated so no new bugs or germs can get into it.

SHOCK THERAPY

Let's say you've had an orchid for three years and it looks great and is getting enough light, but it just won't bloom. Before you throw it out, give it one more chance—you might be able to shock it into bloom. Here are some tips:

TEMPERATURE / If the orchid has been growing in an area that is basically the same temperature all the time, expose the orchid to a few days of major temperature fluctuation, say 20° to 30°F. A thermometer that records maximum and minimum temperatures is a handy way to monitor this. Move the orchid into a room that stays cooler at night, then a room that stays warmer during the day to achieve temperature differentiation. Then wait.

FOOD / Stop using your regular fertilizer and change to a blooming fertilizer (see page 39). Pick a fertilizer with 0 as the first number and fertilize for 3 weeks with this. Then wait.

WATER / Try the old-fashioned trick of watering your beloved plant with slightly warm water for a week. No one is sure why this works, but it often does.

ABUSE / No more Mr. Nice Guy! I met a grower who would drop a stubborn plant on the ground to shake it up. And then the plant would bloom. I prefer to verbally threaten my orchids. But not often, as it makes me feel too guilty.

ARE ORCHIDS POISONOUS?

A host on a reality survival show filmed in the jungles of South America recommended eating the flowers of an *Odontoglossum* species to stave off hunger. I do not recommend this, as there are Oncidium species that are highly hallucinogenic and are used by native peoples for this purpose. We know very, very little about the toxicity of orchids. Though we know that many orchids have been used in traditional folk medicine, this has not been thoroughly investigated. In short, we do not know enough to risk experimentation. So don't eat orchids, and keep them away from pets and young children.

Orchid True and False

Here are ten common beliefs about orchids, some false and some true.

1. *You should water your orchid with ice cubes:* **FALSE.**
   I have been in the jungles where orchids grow and have never seen an ice cube on a branch next to an orchid. I have met people that swear by this method, but I have also seen their plants, which are almost always dehydrated and full of bugs and mites. In theory, water from a melting ice cube is released slowly into the rapidly draining potting medium, but in reality the amount of water that is delivered from an ice cube is inadequate, unless you use two trays of ice on a 6-inch plant. Plus, you are not getting the plant itself wet, which creates a low-humidity situation that sustains pests such as spider mites. The ice also damages the plant tissue where it is placed, and besides, what happens if someone wants a martini? I have tested this method in a home orchid-growing situation. The results were poor.

2. *Orchids should be watered from the bottom:* **FALSE.**
   With this method, the orchid is placed in a deep saucer filled with water, and when the water is gone, the saucer is filled again. But this method simply does not work. The potting medium at the bottom of the pot just gets waterlogged, and any new roots at the

top of the pot receive no water, plus any new roots that do reach the bottom of the pot will quickly rot from so much moisture. The plant might appear to be doing well for a while, but most likely it will rot and suddenly fail.

3. *Orchids should be repotted at night:* **FALSE.**
Again, I understand the reasoning behind this myth: Plants rest at night, so repotting then means less disturbance. But, let's be honest— repotting an orchid in complete darkness is ridiculous, as you can't see what you're doing! And if you turn the light on, the orchid will think it's morning anyway. I never understood this one. Just do your repotting during the day, when it is easiest.

4. *Orchids live forever:* **FALSE.**
There are orchids in botanical collections around the world that are well over a hundred years old, which prompts this myth. But, no, orchids do not live forever. They may live a long time, and there are documented sympodial orchids in cultivation that have lived for over a hundred years, but orchids have a natural life span, just as we do.

5. *Touching orchid flowers can give you flesh-eating bacteria:* **FALSE.**
I think an orchid grower who didn't want people touching his plants must have started this myth. There are a few types of orchids, such as sobralia, whose flowers contain self-digestive enzymes, but those work on the flower tissue only, not on human flesh.

6. *Orchid fragrance can cause you to faint or gag:* **TRUE.**
I have heard of this happening with heavily sweet-scented types such as cattleyas and brassavolas, and I have actually seen it happen with *Dendrochilum magnum.* I displayed a large, flowering orchid in a business office, and the fragrance was so overpowering that two employees were affected, one becoming pale

and giddy, the other nauseous. The employees got the day off, and I had to remove the plant.

7. *You can keep orchids even if you are allergic to pollen:* **TRUE.**
Orchid pollen is massed and attached to the flower, intended to be taken by its specific pollinator, whether bug or bird, and delivered to the next flower. The pollen stays in a solid mass and does not dissipate into the air, so those with pollen allergies will not suffer.

8. *Orchids can beat the odds:* **TRUE.**
More than a few times I have been awed and humbled by the willpower of orchids. I've seen gorgeous orchids thriving despite the fact that they had been growing in the same pot for years and years and had no roots. Others had been burned beyond recognition by the sun, while others had been left outside by mistake for an entire winter, yet were still blooming like crazy. Sometimes, I honestly have no advice to give: orchids have an incredible determination to adapt and survive that never ceases to amaze me.

9. *Orchids are an aphrodisiac:* **MAYBE.**
Historically, both the plant parts and flowers of many orchids have been used as aphrodisiacs, probably because of their resemblance to human sexual organs. The word *orchid* is derived from the Greek word for "testicle," which was instantly apparent when I dug up my first European terrestrial orchid, an orchis, when I was in Greece. In this genus, the root stems have evolved into tubers, usually paired. And there is no denying that many orchid flowers resemble female sexual organs.

In India, a large state-owned company sells an herbal aphrodisiac made from the flowers and stems of *Vanda tessellata,* a traditional medicinal orchid in the East. Salep, made from the orchid tubers of *Orchis mascula* and related species, is used to make a traditional heated drink believed to improve

A stunning Laelia at the San Francisco Conservatory of Flowers.

sexual performance and desire in Europe and the Near East. While science is still investigating these potions I'd like to believe there is some truth to this myth.

The fragrance of some orchid species is also considered to be an aphrodisiac. If you ever spend the night with a *Brassavola nodosa*, you may agree.

10. *There are black orchids:* **TRUE.**

Although they are rare, black orchids do exist, and from the beginning of recorded orchid collecting, they have been pursued. When you look at old orchid flower prints, you will see that the orchids known as black orchids, such as *Coelogyne pandurata* and the *Encyclia* and *Paphiopedilum* species, all had some black in their flowers, usually around the lip, but were rarely completely black. But we do have actual black orchids now; some black-flowered species have been found and are now sold in the marketplace, and orchid hybridizers have produced black paphiopedilums, catasetums, and cymbidiums.

Outdoor Growing Guide

Where you live in the world will determine and define what kinds of orchids can be grown outdoors. For example, if you live in southern Florida, a vanda is an outdoor growing orchid, but if you live in California, vandas will die outside from the cold and need to be grown in the house. If you live in California, your masdevallias can be grown outside, but in Florida, they will wilt in the heat and need an air-conditioned house to grow.

Every region is a bit different for growing orchids outdoors. Many regions, like the western United States, have multiple plant-hardiness zones (a plant's "hardiness" refers to how well it can withstand cold temperatures), so it is important to know the nuances of your region and

which orchids thrive best there before trying to grow them outdoors. The good news is, you can grow healthy orchids almost anywhere as long as you have the proper knowledge and information.

HARDINESS

The United States is divided into eleven different plant-hardiness zones, determined by average minimum temperature. This is primarily what growers use to determine which orchids can grow outside where, so find out what zone you are in. (See www.garden.org for a map of growing zones in the States.) In zones 1 to 7, where it is very cold during the winter, with the temperature well below freezing, only the hardiest of orchids can survive outdoors. The good news is that the selection of orchids that can survive a snowy winter is ever increasing as orchid producers are developing more rugged orchids for the marketplace.

In zone 8, more tropical orchids like cymbidiums can be grown. By zone 9, the variety widens, with orchids like Australian dendrobiums being able to brave the winters, and by zone 10 you may not be able to find room for the variety of orchids that will grow. By zone 11, the jungle is yours.

The rest of the world is divided into plant hardiness zones as well. I have seen cymbidiums growing outside in common hardiness zones in Crete, England, and Australia. And more and more types of orchids for outdoor growing in the colder hardiness zones are being produced and developed and entering the world marketplace. It is just a matter of time before the brilliant European and Asian hardy terrestrial orchids will be available to us here in the United States, and our beautiful terrestrial lady slipper orchids will be found in gardens in other parts of the world.

CLIMATE

It is important to keep in mind that plant hardiness zones are based on average low temperatures

Orchids growing outdoors in the Midwest.

and have nothing to do with climate factors like humidity levels, weather patterns, and amount of rainfall. Given that humidity is so important in orchid growth and cultivation, it is essential to know about your climate as well. For example, foggy summers in and near San Francisco in zone 10 are not the same as zone 10 in Florida. Go to www.garden.org/zipzone to enter your zip code and find out about the plant hardiness in your own specific climate.

Remember, you cannot just cast your orchids outside; you must take note of the low and high temperatures, sun exposure, climate, fluctuating weather patterns, watering needs, and potential predators. Be sure to do your research first. Your orchids are not protected against summer hail and marauding wild pigs. If you plan to grow outdoors, talk to your local grower or seller about the best orchids for the hardiness zone and climate of your region.

TIPS FOR GROWING ORCHIDS OUTDOORS

There are three basic environmental scenarios for outdoor orchid growing:

1. *Growing orchids outside year-round in zones 2 to 7:* This is where our native hardy orchids live naturally, and you can introduce newly developed types of hardy orchids like bletilla to your garden. I recommend that you follow the growing instructions given to you when you purchase the plant, as in this case there is no expert as good as your local expert.

2. *Growing orchids outside year-round in zones 8 to 11:* This is where orchids from tropical regions, either cool-growing or warm-growing, will thrive.

3. *Growing orchids outside in the summer, in all zones:* When conditions are favorable, any orchid will appreciate some time growing outside. Orchid growers call this "summering" your orchids.

If you decide to move your orchid outdoors for the summer, it is best to do so in the spring, or when night temperatures stay above 55°F. You must remember that all orchids need a gradual exposure to increased sunlight, and will burn immediately if exposed to direct sunlight for the first time. If you do not have a shady location for your plant, create one with a patio umbrella or shade cloth. You can also make a tent out of layered cheesecloth: Place your orchid on a perforated surface such as a bench, a milk crate, or a slatted box to ensure drainage. If humidity is low in your area, you can place a pan or an edged tarp under the bench so that the water can puddle to increase humidity. If bugs are a real problem, make a little house with shade cloth covering the floor as well. A water mister is also a good idea if you have low humidity. If you use a mister along with a simple watering timer, you can create nearly perfect conditions.

As the summer begins to cool, keep a close eye on your plant and the nighttime temperature. When the nighttime temperature drops to 55°F, it is time to bring your orchid back inside. Carefully examine the plant and pot for any bugs and snails before bringing it indoors. You do not want uninvited company.

NATURAL FERTILIZER

Orchids do not require as much fertilizer when grown outside and sometimes do not seem to need any at all. I have also noticed that orchids grown outside seem to be more sensitive to applied fertilizer; their root tips are more susceptible to burning and other damage, and their leaves are more likely to accumulate salt and fertilizer residues. When you do fertilize your outdoor orchids, I recommend diluting the fertilizer an extra 50 percent.

INDICATOR PLANTS

If you are not sure what types of orchids will thrive outside in your neighborhood, take a look around for non-orchid plants that can act as a temperature indicator. For example, in the West (hardiness zone 10), tree ferns, jacaranda trees, and cycad palms indicate a good temperature for growing common types of orchids for that region and hardiness. For zones 9 and 10, eucalyptus trees, fuchsias, bougainvilleas, and royal palms are good indicators. For zones 7 and 8, indicators include English holly, pittosporums, and rhododendrons. For zones 5 and 6, look for Japanese maple, flowering dogwood, California privet, and English yew; for zones 3 and 4, sugar maple, Boston ivy, Virginia creeper, and Japanese yew.

THE HARDIEST OUTDOOR ORCHID

I have always been impressed with the hardiness of the *Bletilla striata* orchid. Besides growing and doing well in the San Francisco Bay Area, it also grows in Sacramento, California, which is freezing in the winter and blazing hot in the summer. Over the years, I've seen it growing outside in Hawaii, Georgia, Ohio, and Florida, and recently I have learned that it also grows outside in Oklahoma, North Carolina, Pennsylvania, Texas, New Jersey, Connecticut, and most points in between. Talk about versatile. Because of its growing popularity and exposure, orchid producers and plant nurseries have started to increase production of both the species and newly introduced hybrids, increasing the varieties and the color selection available.

Bletilla striata is one tough orchid.

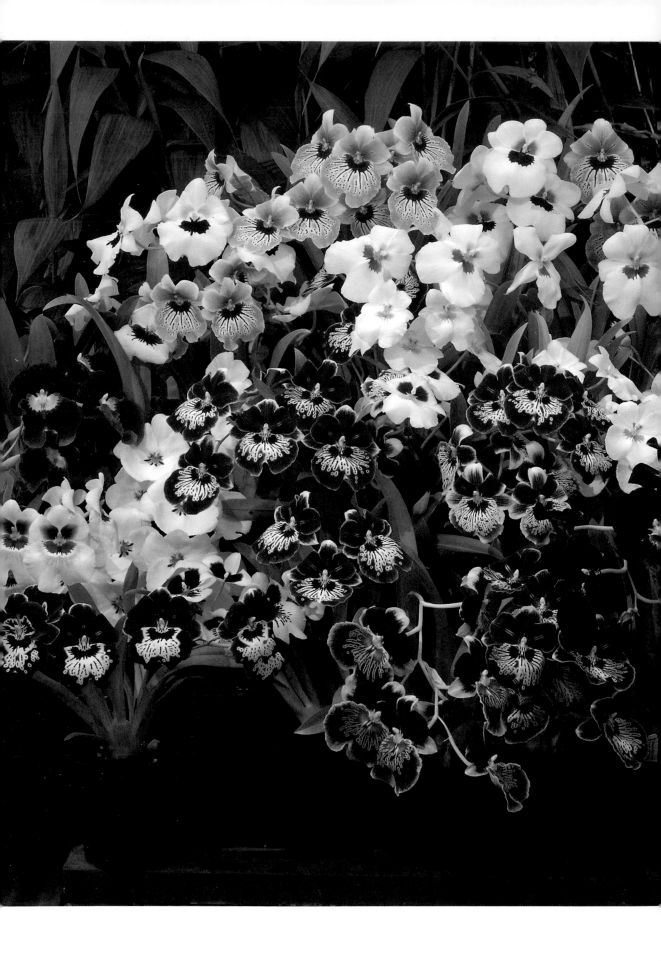

Part Three

EXPERT TIPS
FOR EASY-TO-GROW
ORCHIDS

THE TWELVE MOST POPULAR ORCHIDS

The ever-growing popularity of orchids in the United States and the world is driving orchid producers to introduce more different types of orchids to the marketplace. I have seen more new types of orchids introduced in the past five years than in the previous twenty years. This is a good thing, as it means more diversity and more accessibility to orchids that would have cost a fortune just ten years ago.

Here are twelve of the most popular orchids commonly available today. Because these orchids are fairly easy to grow, they are good choices for novice and experienced growers alike.

Phalaenopsis

The most popular orchid in the world today and deservedly so, the phalaenopsis is extremely adaptable to almost any environment. Commonly known as phals, these plants have a rich history, both in their native lands of Southeast Asia and northern Australia, and in their early discovery and appreciation in cultures around the world. The word *phalaenopsis* means "mothlike" in Greek, and refers to the large flowers that look like hovering moths. I have grown phals for years and am a great fan of their elegance and purity of form. A phalaenopsis will create tranquility in any setting, from a busy shoe store to the most regal of homes. I choose them often for display, due to their long-lasting and dependable flowering and their strong growth. The great thing about the mass production and popularity of phals is that today's hybrids are as tough as nails. They also come in an ever-increasing color variety, with spots and stripe combinations that get better each year, and they can flower for months. Yellow, brown, gold, red, and green flowers now join the classic white or pink phalaenopsis, and we can expect more colors to come. Some species of phals have leaves that are mottled with red and silver, which makes the plants attractive even when not in flower. Amazingly, growers have cut the seed-to-bloom time of these orchids from seven years to two years. You will never get bored with a phal.

Phalaenopsis hybrids bring new colors and patterns.

❖ **GROWING CONDITIONS**
Phals are a warm-climate orchid from the steamy jungles of Southeast Asia, but they will live happily in your home as long as the temperature stays between 58° and 75°F.

A traditional white phalaenopsis

The vast majority of phals sold in today's marketplace are planted in sphagnum moss. But many growers still use the trustworthy large-size orchid bark, while others are excited about using the new redwood fiber. I recommend all three, as each has proven its worth, and phalaenopsis roots love them all. The three kinds of potting medium differ in water retention ability, with orchids grown in orchid bark drying out quicker than those grown in moss and redwood fiber, so choose according to your personal preference and commitment to maintenance.

Phals are famously easy to grow in the home. They defy growing logic and adapt and grow and bloom beautifully almost anywhere, making them perfect for beginners. In nature, phals are shade-loving plants. This is primarily why they make such great houseplants; they grow well in a shady to bright room without direct sunlight.

For your phals, pick a location in a room that is bright and humid. Kitchens and bathrooms are a good choice, as they tend to have the best humidity. Avoid strong direct sunlight. Phal leaves are easily burned, so keep an eye on the changing position of the sun.

✣ WATERING

The size of the pot your phal is growing in, what kind of mix your phal is planted in, and the time of the year all factor into how often your orchid should be watered. The best way to determine the watering cycle of your phal is to check its weight. You want the plant to dry out between waterings, but you don't want it to get completely bone dry. Achieving this balance is easy to do once you have determined the watering cycle of your plant. (See "All-Natural Tips for Orchid Care," page 48, for more information on watering.)

Water your orchid thoroughly in the sink, getting both sides of the leaves wet. Water splashed on the flowers will not hurt them; just be sure the water drains off or evaporates quickly. After watering, tip the plant from side to side to drain out any water that has collected in the crown of the phal and between the leaves. Blowing into the crown to blow out the water helps as well.

✣ FERTILIZING

I recommend fertilizing phals weekly year-round with a half-strength (diluted 50 percent more than what is recommended on the package) 20-10-10 fertilizer. The roots on these orchids tend to grow rather wildly, so be sure that they are receiving the fertilizer. Do not get carried away and feed this plant too often, or unattractive salts will form on the top of the leaves, and the root tips may burn.

Changing to a 0-10-10 blooming fertilizer when a new flower spike first appears can result in larger and usually more flowers, but I recommend using this for only a couple of months and switching back to regular fertilizer as soon as a new leaf starts to grow, even if there are flowers left on the plant.

✣ REPOTTING

When phals are growing well, you will see the silvery white aerial roots growing out of the top and sometimes bottom of the pot. This is normal, although it can be a little disconcerting if your phal's roots have attached themselves to other objects, such as the table. The best time to repot phals is when you see new roots with green tips emerging at the base of the phal.

To repot, water the plant and allow it to drain. If the phal is growing in a plastic pot, it is best to squeeze the pot a little from opposite sides, and then rotate and squeeze the other two sides. This helps to loosen the roots from the plastic pot so only a minimal amount of root damage occurs. If the phal is growing in a clay pot, it sometimes helps to invert the pot, allowing some of the potting mixture to fall out, then turn the plant back over and use a small kitchen knife to gently pry the roots loose (see page 34). Holding the base of the plant, slowly and gently pull the phal from its pot until it is free.

✦ TIPS FOR REBLOOMING

Typically, a mature phal growing in a house establishes a rhythm of blooming, producing a new leaf, and after the leaf, a new flower spike, and blooming again, and this takes between ten to fourteen months. A new orchid fresh from a greenhouse will have to acclimate to your house, so don't be alarmed if it takes a little longer to bloom a second time.

MORE TIPS FOR PHALAENOPSIS

ARCHED PHALAENOPSIS / Phals used for display purposes often have a flower spike that arches perfectly downward to create a vertical flower display. You can wire your phal to assume almost any shape you want, from blooming straight up and down to gracefully arching over that Buddha head in your living room. Phal flower spikes are surprisingly flexible; all you need is some medium-grade floral wire and some wire twist ties.

First, buy a phal with the fewest number of flowers opened. Using the flower spike as a sizing guide, bend the wire to the shape you wish to achieve, in this case a pronounced arch. Slowly start bending the spike and attaching the stem to the wire every inch or two as needed, being careful not to break off any flower buds. You do not want to tie the spike too tightly. Continue around the arch, and as you get to the end of the spike, where it is thinner, wire only if needed. After just two to six days, you can carefully remove everything and the newly arched spike will keep its arched shape.

A phalaenopsis straight from the store with natural flower spike arch.

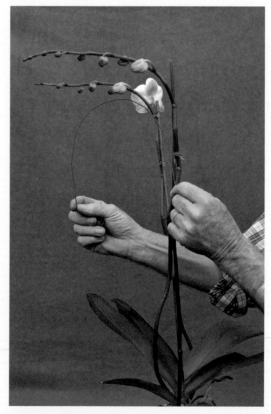

Bend floral wire to desired arch.

After just two or three days, carefully remove all clips and wire, and the flower spike will retain the form.

HOW TO LENGTHEN YOUR PHAL'S BLOOM-ING SEASON / Almost all commercially produced phals have the ability to send additional flower spikes branching off of the main flower spike. Some phals will do this naturally when mature and growing well. Phals blooming for over a year are not uncommon. To encourage a phal to branch, cut off the tip of the flower spike before the last flower on the flower spike dies. From the tip of the flower spike, count three to five flower nodes (where the flower attaches to the spike) in and cut the spike there. You will see new flower spikes emerging from the old spike after a week or two. And this is how we keep our phals blooming. (Although usually by the third cut, the plant is really tired and you should give it a break and just leave it alone by cutting the spike off completely at the base.)

Another reason to just leave a green flower spike on the plant even though there are no more flowers is that sometimes baby plants, or keikis, will form on the ends of the spikes. Leave these keikis on the stem until they have made at least three roots, at which time they can be cut from the spike and potted in their own pot.

If the whole flower spike is brown and dead, cut it off as close to the base of the spike as possible.

FRAGRANT PHALAENOPSIS

Fragrance is a weak gene in the phalaenopsis world. Most of the large, multiflowered hybrid types that are so popular carry no fragrance whatsoever, but this will be changing in the coming years as growers cater to the popularity of fragrance. Many new hybrids of the miniature phalaenopsis type are fragrant and are now being offered in the marketplace:

Phal. amabilis
Phal. cornu-cervi
Phal. fascieta
Phal. gigantea
Phal. lueddemanniana
Phal. pulchra
Phal. stuartiana

Cattleya

Named in 1821 in honor of William Cattley, one of the earliest English tropical orchid growers, this is commonly referred to as the king of orchids. This is your grandmother's orchid, your mother's prom flower, the flower used as a pattern for everything from silverware to polo shirts. Found in the New World from Mexico to South America, it continues to be one of the world's most beloved orchids.

Cattleya mossiae is in my list of top-five all-time favorite orchids. Few things either in nature or the manmade world can match the beauty and fragrance of this plant. Cattleyas can grow large and take up a lot of space in the home. Today, they are bred to be smaller, and only a handful of growers still produce the larger size. Cattleya species are divided into two groups, the unifoliates, which have one leaf and large flowers, and the bifoliates, which have two leaves or sometimes more per stem. The bifoliate type includes the largest and tallest catts, with smaller flowers. Both types are very

A cattleya hybrid starting to grow out of the pot.

fragrant and fun to grow. Because it is one of the most hybridized orchids to be found, the color selection is huge, from bright oranges, reds, and pastels to the classic purples and pinks, as well as rarer colors such as greens, browns, and even blues.

✤ GROWING CONDITIONS

Cattleyas grow well in warm to intermediate 55° to 85°F household temperatures, and are easy to grow and bloom in the home. They enjoy high light levels, but not direct sun. Keep them in your brightest room. Great drainage is mandatory, as they will quickly rot and dehydrate in stale and soggy potting media.

✤ WATERING

When growing cattleyas in the house, it is important to have a watering schedule, especially when growing them in clay pots, as it is harder then to gauge when they are dry. If the plant is in a 6-inch clay pot, you should water a minimum of once a week. With a smaller hybrid growing in a plastic pot, the best way to gauge when the plant needs watering is by picking it up to judge the weight and watering when light in weight. When you are watering, inspect the plant for both active growth and plump bulbs. When a plant is actively growing, the pot will dry out twice as fast, and sometimes this growth coincides with the colder months when the heat is on so you want to make sure it gets a lot of water. Dehydrated or shriveled bulbs indicate that the plant is not getting enough water.

✤ FERTILIZING

Use a 20-10-10 fertilizer for your cattleya, applying it with each watering while the plant is growing new roots and foliage. Once the new leaf and bulb are formed, scale down to half-strength. If new roots with green tips are

A classic cattleya hybrid

emerging from the bulb, use half-strength fertilizer to avoid burning the new root tips.

✤ REPOTTING

Repot only when new green growth and new roots appear at the base of the plant. Ideally, this will coincide with the development of new roots about an inch long under the new growth.

Before you repot, give the plant a good watering. If the cattleya is growing in a clay pot, you might find that the roots have strongly affixed themselves to the clay. If this is the case, take a thin dinner knife, slip it between the root(s) and the pot, gently pry off all the roots, and remove the plant from the pot. If the catt is in a plastic pot, squeezing the pot will be enough to loosen some of the roots, but cattleya roots are tenacious so you might need to use a knife to pry them all off the plastic. Gently remove all the old potting medium and cut off the dead roots as close to the bottom of the rhizome at the base of the bulb as possible. If the oldest bulbs are dead, cut the bulbs and rhizomes off where the live growth begins. If the root system is large and healthy, select a pot that will allow for two years of new growth (meaning room for the rhizome to produce two more bulbs). If there are few roots, use a smaller pot allowing for just a year's growth.

To repot, use one hand to hold the plant suspended in space inside the pot, with the bottom of the bulbs about ½ inch below the top of the pot. Using your other hand, distribute wet fresh potting medium equally around the plant, tapping it down as you go and making sure that you do not cover the rhizome or new growth. Water the plant after repotting until the water drains clear and free of debris.

✤ TIPS ON REBLOOMING

As your new cattleya growth matures, you will notice a flower sheath forming at the end of the bulb at the base of the leaf. This is where the new flower spike will emerge. If this sheath starts to yellow before you can see the new flower spike forming, this could indicate bud or sheath blasting, which means that a rapid temperature change outside of the sheath has caused condensation to form within the sheath, where it will rot the newly forming flower spike. To fix this, you must carefully tear or cut the sheath away without damaging the flower buds and spike within.

Lady's Slipper

Lady's slipper orchids, so named for the large, pouch that resembles an old-fashioned lady's slipper, contain three genera of orchids that can be grown in the home, though they are all grown much differently: paphiopedilums, phragmipediums, and cypripediums.

Prized since Victorian days, when orchid hunters combed the tropics to find new species, destroying what they could not take and keeping the locations secret from others, lady's slipper orchids still seem to bring out the worst in some people. They are still sought, stolen, and smuggled from national parks and protected biosystems, and were the first orchids to be listed in the endangered-orchid index.

PAPHIOPEDILUM

The name comes from Paphos, a Greek city with numerous temples to Venus, and *pedilum*, the Greek word for "slipper." This tropical warm-growing orchid from the region of eastern Asia is the most popular type of lady's slipper. Resilient and easy to grow in the home, paphs are probably the easiest orchids to rebloom, or at least to keep alive. I have seen paphs rebloom even when the orchid was down to one miserable-looking leaf.

❖ GROWING CONDITIONS
The majority of commercial paphs sold are low-light-loving orchids and grow well at household temperatures of 60° to 90°F. When I visit homes where orchids are grown, the oldest orchids in the collection are usually paphiopedilums. I have had some of my own paphs for over twenty years. Pick a moderately bright, warm room for these orchids, out of any direct sunlight.

❖ WATERING
Because of the absence of any water-retaining pseudobulbs, these orchids should be kept

A modern paphiopedilum hybrid, one of the longest-lasting flowers in the orchid world.

constantly moist. Be careful to keep water out of the crown of the plant. Water can collect in the natural depression formed by the arching new leaf, and if coupled with low air circulation, it can cause this tender new growth to rot. Simply take a moment after watering to tilt the pot, allowing the excess water to drain out. You can also blow on the crown to disperse the water.

❖ FERTILIZING
Fertilize these plants with a 20-20-20 fertilizer year-round twice per month. If you would rather fertilize with your weekly waterings, use a 10-10-10 fertilizer mix.

❖ REPOTTING
I have seen paphiopedilums grow successfully in every kind of potting medium available in the marketplace. They do not seem to have a

A cheerful group of paphiopedilums

preference, but I do, and I have found this mix to work splendidly: two parts fine bark mixed with one part fine perlite and charcoal mixed 50-50. I will sometimes add 1 teaspoon of crushed natural oyster shell, as that seems to aid flowering. I prefer to use plastic pots with multiple drainage holes at the bottom (see picture, page 32), as these pots retain water well while affording excellent drainage. I know very few paphiopedilum growers who use clay pots.

✤ TIPS FOR REBLOOMING
Paphiopedilums are easy-to-bloom orchids as long as the plants are healthy and have a good root system. Check frequently to see if the plant is secure in its pot and the root system is sound. If not, repot. For stubborn-blooming plants, try applying a blooming fertilizer (see page 39) in the early spring months. If you have no luck with that, move the plant to a cooler, brighter location in the house for a week, then return it to its original location.

PHRAGMIPEDIUM

This South American slipper orchid group has been getting a lot of attention over the past dozen years with the discovery of a beautiful bright orange species, *Phrag. besseae*, and just a few years ago the discovery of the huge purple-flowered species, *Phrag. kovachii*. Generally requiring a little more water and a little less heat than paphiopedilums, phrags are also easy to grow and flower dependably.

This interesting plant group also contains *Phragmipedium caudatum*, the "mustache," or "Mandarin," lady slipper, which has petals up to 3 feet long. The name *Phragmipedium* comes from the Greek *phragma*, meaning "fence" or "ridge," and *pedium*, meaning "slipper" again, referring to the ridged divisions inside the flower's pouch.

✤ GROWING CONDITIONS
These orchids should be grown at temperatures between 55° and 85°F, a little cooler than

Phragmipediums, once hard to find, are now prominent in the marketplace.

paphiopedilums and with a little more light. They also enjoy fresh air, so be sure there is good air circulation. They like to be potted in smaller pots with good drainage.

✤ WATERING
Because they have no bulbs to store water, phragmapediums should never be allowed to dry out completely. I recommend keeping them on the wet side, especially since they are generally grown in small pots, which dry out faster. There are growers who grow them in saucers and allow the plant to sit in water that is emptied and replaced with every watering, which is unusual culture for any orchid. I am not wild about this approach, and while I have seen phrags grown this way that look great, I do not recommend it, as you are courting disaster should rot appear or you forget to change the water in the saucer.

✤ FERTILIZING
Fertilize these just as you would your *paphiopedilums*: year-round with 20-20-20 fertilizer

twice per month, or a 10-10-10 fertilizer with your weekly waterings.

✤ REPOTTING

Repot a phragmipedium using a fine bark and perlite mix, when you see new growth appearing at the base of the plant. I sometimes add a fine-grade lava rock (available at nurseries) to help with drainage. Pot in small (3- to 6-inch) pots, never more than 1 to 2 inches larger than the previous pot, making sure the plant is secure by tapping and pushing the potting medium down. This orchid will take forever to send out new roots and growth if it is the least bit wobbly in the pot.

✤ TIPS FOR REBLOOMING

If the orchid fails to bloom, try moving it to a brighter, cooler location. If it still doesn't bloom, add blooming fertilizer in early spring.

CYPRIPEDIUM

America's lady's slipper orchid grows outside in almost every state in zones 2 through 9 (see "Outdoor Growing Guide," page 54), with the widest variety found in the coldest states. Thus, it can be grown outside year-round in North America and in northern latitudes around the world. The name comes from the Greek word *cyp*, referring to the island of Cyprus, and *pedium*, again meaning "slipper." Orchid growers are starting to grow and hybridize cypripedium, as it is a true hardy orchid and demand is increasing due to success with it in the garden. Unfortunately, many species both in America and in Europe are close to extinction due to overcollecting and land development.

Historically, this orchid was thought of as tricky to grow both indoors and outdoors, and it's true that at one time they were hard to propagate. But today's producers have worked out those problems, and plants are successfully grown all over the world. The orchids are sold in an advanced stage of growth, ready to be planted

Cypripediums, America's lady's slipper.

in your garden. It is just a matter of time until this group hits the mainstream marketplace.

✤ GROWING CONDITIONS

Cypripediums prefer shade. Although they do enjoy morning sun, noontime sun should be avoided, and they should be exposed to only filtered sun in the afternoon. Plant in the cool part of your garden in raised beds of sand and loam- or leaf-based compost. Drainage must be excellent, so consider putting gravel at the base of the beds, at an angle to be sure the water drains down or out. If planting in pots, use the same potting medium and grow in heavier shade. Almost all cypripediums are resistant to winter frost and snow when they are in their dormant stage, which is after blooming and growing when the leaves fall off and all that remains is the rhizome.

✤ WATERING

Water cypripediums heavily in the spring. After flowering, the plants will die back and watering can be reduced.

Phaphiopedilums are growing in popularity as new and impressive hybrids are being produced.

✤ FERTILIZING

You need to be careful fertilizing cypripediums because their roots are very sensitive. I recommend fertilizing once a month using a 10-10-10 fertilizer at half the recommended strength. Do not fertilize at all during winter.

✤ REPOTTING

This is one of the few orchids that likes to be potted; it can be kept for several years in the same pot. (If grown in the ground and left undisturbed, it will quickly grow into large clumps.) The best time to repot is late summer or early autumn, when the plant is entering its dormant stage. You must clean the plant completely so that it is free of all debris, including the dry old growth. Pot the roots and rhizomes using a coarse well-draining mix of sand and loam (regular garden compost). Adding perlite to the mix will bring good results as well. Plant in a pot that is no more than 1 to 2 inches larger than the previous pot.

✤ TIPS FOR REBLOOMING

If your cyp isn't blooming, try moving it to another cool location with a different exposure. I've had success reblooming stubborn plants using a commercial daylily blooming fertilizer, available at nurseries.

Oncidium

Oncidiums are now so common in Asia that many think they are from there, but they actually originate from tropical America.

Oncidiums hail from the New World, ranging from Mexico to Peru. Oncidiums made a big first impression on me in the early days of my orchid career. I bought one oncidium plant cheap and out of bloom, and I grew it by a sliding glass door, where it got a lot of good morning light. About a year later, I noticed a flower spike first emerging from the side of the bulb, already about an inch long. I checked its progress daily, and about a month later, the flower spike had grown to an amazing 3 feet tall, and a few weeks after that I had swarms of sun-bright yellow flowers cascading above my reading chair. I was hooked on oncidiums forever.

Oncidiums are commonly called "dancing ladies," because the flowers look like yellow-skirted dancers, especially when flitting around in a breeze. Their name is taken from the Greek word *onkos*, meaning "torso," referring to the pad-like growth that appears on the lip of each flower, forming the torso of the "lady." There is great diversity in this group: some oncidiums are smaller than your thumb, with spikes 6 inches tall and even growing to over 12 feet tall! There are species like *Oncidium lancifolium* that have very small bulbs with a single thick leaf resembling a horse's ear; these are called mule ear oncidiums. The entire plant of one species can be smaller than the flower of another. This is an exciting and rewarding orchid to grow, and new types are constantly entering the marketplace.

✤ GROWING CONDITIONS

The most popular groups of oncidiums, the common yellow-flowered types you see everywhere, are also the easiest to grow. These plants like to be grown in warmer temperatures, up to about 90°F, and will slow down at 50°F, stop growing at 40°F, and become damaged or die when in the low 30s for any length of time. They love a little sun in the morning and afternoon and will bloom easily in a house with very bright light. They also thrive in a well-ventilated space with good air movement. The base species used in modern hybrids are *Onc. flexuosm* and *Onc. varicosum*. Both of these species have a natural climbing habit, and their hybrids will grow and climb right out of the pot and up the nearest wall. For this reason, oncidiums do better in net or wire baskets with a fine-bark and perlite mix, or mounted on tree fern or cork slabs (see "Mounting Orchids," page 42), which mimics how they are found growing on trees and branches in their natural habitat.

The yellow lip, or "dress" in these oncidium "dancing lady" flowers is growing in size with every new hybrid as breeders strive to make them ever larger and brighter.

❖ WATERING

When actively growing, oncidiums will take all the water you give them, so water as often as you can at first. Once the new bulb is fat and mature, you should cut the watering down and try to give them a slightly longer dry period. This technique generally results in a higher flower count and helps to keep the potting medium from going stale.

❖ FERTILIZING

These orchids do well with a weekly 20-10-10 fertilizer mix at three-fourths the recommended strength all year round. The roots of oncidiums are particularly susceptible to fertilizer burn, so never use a full-strength mix.

❖ REPOTTING

Because of their climbing growing habit, oncidiums almost always look like they need repotting because they are constantly climbing out of the pots with their roots all over the place. A good way to determine if they really do need repotting is to check and see if the new roots are entering the potting medium as they cascade down from the point of new growth. If they are, things are fine for the time being. If the new roots are avoiding the medium, this tells you that the potting medium has rotted or soured and the plant should be repotted. Water the plant before beginning and then remove the plant from the old pot, discarding the old potting medium. Cut off all the dead roots as close to the rhizome as possible. The new growth with the healthy roots will have climbed above the previous level of the pot and now must be buried in the new medium. As long as you have removed all the dead roots, the bulb will be content buried there.

❖ TIPS FOR REBLOOMING

The primary cause of oncidiums failing to rebloom is lack of sufficient light. So, move your plant to a brighter location or a location that gets an hour or two of early morning sun.

FRAGRANT ONCIDIUMS

There is something about coming home and smelling your orchid before you see it that makes me a believer in orchids. The oncidium group contains types with my favorite fragrances. In my opinion, *Oncidium* Sharry Baby is the best modern fragrant orchid in the market today. You can smell it as soon as you step inside your house. Another great fragrant oncidium is *Onc. cheirophorum.* This smaller orchid has a very sweet, dominant scent that has led to many new oncidium hybrids in yellow, pink, and white, including Twinkle, *Miltonidium* Pupukea Sunset, and Gold Dust. (See page 137 for a list of fragrant orchids.)

Oncidium chrysomorphum has smaller flowers than most oncidiums but carries a lovely citrus scent.

ONCIDIUM HYBRIDS: WILSONARAS, MILTONIDIUMS, ODONTOCIDIUMS, BRASSIDIUMS

With their ease of growth, adaptability, and great flowering habit, oncidiums obviously have much to offer. Orchid breeders have long recognized this and have crossed oncidiums with other types to create "improved" plants. This is now the most rapidly growing group of orchids in today's marketplace. Crossing oncidiums with other orchids has given us strong plants in an ever-increasing selection of colors and shapes.

ONCIDIUM HYBRIDS IN THE MARKETPLACE

ONCIDIUM + MILTONIA = MILTONIDIUM
Small- to medium-size flowers, purple or yellow in color, occasionally fragrant

ONCIDIUM + ODONTOGLOSSUM = ODONTOCIDIUM
Tall, large flowers, white or red in color

ONCIDIUM + BRASSIA = BRASSIDIUM
Tall yellow or brown flowers

ONCIDIUM + COCHLIODA + ODONTGLOSSUM = WILSONARA
Brightly colored flowers; tall spikes; occasionally fragrant

ONCIDIUM + MILTONIA + COCHLIODA + ODONTOGLOSSUN = BURRAGEARA
Tall spikes with multiple flowers in a variety of colors

ONCIDIUM + ODONTOGLOSSUM + BRASSIA = MACLELLANARA
Very large yellow flowers on tall spikes

ONCIDIUM + MILTONIA + BRASSIA = ALICEARA
Pink or brown flowers on mid-size spikes

❖ GROWING CONDITIONS
This diverse group of orchids likes household temperatures of 55° to 85°F. They generally thrive in areas a bit shadier than regular oncidiums, and they will appreciate any humidity you can give them.

❖ WATERING
This group grows in smaller pots, so you should water by weight, as explained in "Watering," page 65. When they are actively growing, they drink a lot of water, so your 4-inch pot might need multiple waterings a week.

❖ FERTILIZING
Use a 20-20-20 fertilizer at the recommended strength every two weeks on oncidium hybrids. Fertilize weekly when the plant is actively growing and new roots are present.

❖ REPOTTING
Repotting is best done with this group after the flowers have finished growing and when new growth is present. Water the plant before repotting. Slip the plant out of its pot, removing all the old potting medium, and cut off all the dead growth, being sure to trim any dead roots as close to the rhizome as possible. Use a pot just large enough for two years of new growth and, holding the plant suspended over the pot, fill it with a mix of four parts fine bark and one part large-size perlite. Tap the medium down and make sure the new growth remains above the level of the medium. Water the plant and make sure it is draining properly, then place it in a shady location for two weeks before returning it to its bright location.

❖ TIPS FOR REBLOOMING
As with regular oncidiums, these plants will rebloom automatically if cared for properly. If the new growth is much smaller than the previous growth, make a point of being careful with your watering, fertilizing, light, and air circulation to get it to bloom again.

Miltoniopsis

A well-grown miltoniopsis

This beautiful orchid looks like a pansy, smells like a rose, and reblooms quickly, so it is no wonder that it has exploded in popularity. The name refers to the similarity of its flowers to the flowers of the genus *Miltonia*, which was named in honor of Earl Fitzwilliam, Viscount Milton, a famous Victorian English orchid grower. The stunning miltoniopsis comes from South America, mostly Columbia, Ecuador, and Peru. The plants we see in the marketplace today are new hybrids that have been bred to be tough and more tolerant of warm conditions.

❖ GROWING CONDITIONS

These orchids are not hard to grow, but when new growth begins at the base of the plant, they need more care and you must make sure to give them enough water. They grow best in a very bright room in as cool a spot as possible, ideally between 50° to 80°F. In warmer climates, some people choose to grow this orchid near the floor, as temperatures are a bit cooler there. The trick to good cultivation of this plant is to identify and cater to the plant's growth pattern; once you do, you will have success in both blooming and growing.

❖ WATERING

The miltoniopsis orchids are grown and sold in smaller-size plastic pots. When flowering, it should be watered enough so that the pot does not become dry (if the plant is carrying a lot of flowers, this can be as often as every four days). As the flowering wanes, the plant needs less water. In one to four weeks, you will notice new growth and roots at the base of the bulb that flowered. As these new roots and growth emerge, the plant will need more water and should be kept moist; water at least twice a week.

❖ FERTILIZING

Fertilize miltoniopsis when you see new roots and plants growing. Use a 20-20-20 fertilizer at 50 percent less than the recommended dose on the package. Fertilize every time you water, skipping every fourth week to avoid damage and salt buildup.

❖ REPOTTING

For the best results, repot miltoniopsis every year after the plant flowers and new growth and new roots appear.

Water the plant before you begin. Let it drain and gently squeeze the corners of the pot to release the plant and root-ball. After removing, gently wash away any potting medium from the roots until they are exposed and clean. Look at the roots closely—the old, dead roots from the older growth should be cut away with scissors. Cut the dead roots off as close to the bulbs as possible. The root systems on miltoniopsis are not as large as those of other types of orchids, so after trimming you won't be left with many roots. Miltoniopsis like to be repotted into small pots, so pick a pot that is large enough to allow for just one year's growth. If the root system is healthy, you can use a slightly larger pot to allow for two years' growth.

This miltoniopsis with its spotted lip is known as a waterfall pattern type.

Water after repotting and note the weight of the plant so you can tell when it needs water again. You must not allow a miltoniopsis at this stage of growth to dry out.

✤ TIPS FOR REBLOOMING

If you follow the guidelines above, miltoniopsis is a dependable bloomer. If the plant has good-looking bulbs but no flowers, move it to a cooler location with a bit more light, and water it in the very early morning or late afternoon to help keep the roots cool.

FRAGRANT MILTONIOPSIS

If you're looking for a fragrant miltoniopsis, be sure to do your shopping before noon. These orchids are generally fragrant only in the morning. By afternoon or evening, they may not have any fragrance at all. (Miltoniopsis with yellow flowers are an exception; they retain some scent throughout the day, although fragrance is still stronger in the morning.)

A MILTONIOPSIS TIP

Leaf crimping—when the leaves remain small and fold onto themselves like an accordion—accompanied with small bulbs can be a symptom of under-watering for most orchids, but for miltoniopsis it usually means that the plant needs repotting. Leaf crimping happens when the roots from the new growth come into contact with soggy and nondraining potting medium and the root tips die, stunting them and making them unable to hydrate the plant properly.

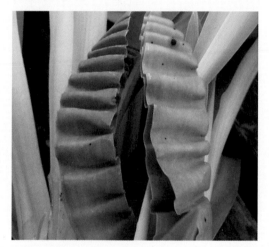

Crimped leaves on the new growth of a miltoniopsis

Vanda

Vandas are easy to grow and bloom with plentiful light.

Being from Northern California, where vandas are not known for flourishing, I've always considered them to be a big deal. Generally expensive and hard to find, they are coveted around the world, and their huge and long-lasting flowers are quite impressive.

The name *vanda* is a Sanskrit word referring to a sacred mistletoe and given to the *Vanda tessellata*, an orchid species found in India. Vandas can be found throughout tropical Asia, into the Philippines, and down to Australia.

This warm-growing tropical orchid is grown in the millions throughout Asia and in America, with the major commercial producers in Florida and Hawaii. The color range of the flowers increases every year as more types are developed.

Most vandas sold today come in either pots or wood slat boxes that allow their roots to hang down; they do well when grown as a hanging plant.

❖ GROWING CONDITIONS

Very bright, very hot (60° to 90°F), and very wet describe the ideal growing conditions for vandas. Pick your warmest, sunniest room for this plant, and a location that allows for frequent watering.

❖ WATERING

Vandas produce thick aerial roots on the stem above the pot. You must be sure to water these. With vandas, it is very important to water all the roots, both in and out of the pot. You will need to water it somewhere where you can use a hose (or shower) so that you can drench the entire plant. Like most orchids, vandas prefer lukewarm water to cold water.

❖ FERTILIZING

Fertilize twice monthly year-round with a 20-20-20 mix as recommended. Be sure to get the solution on both the bottom roots and the aerial roots.

❖ REPOTTING

The vanda is a monopodial orchid, which means that the new growth continually emerges from the top of the plant (see page 47 for more information). The stems and roots will slowly die off. Remove the dead stems and roots regularly.

To repot, water the plant, remove it from the pot slowly (being careful not to break any roots), and then clean off any residual potting medium. Cut off any dead stems and roots, starting from the bottom of the plant. If the aerial roots have died, cut them off as well. Vandas repot well when they have at least three good, healthy silver-colored roots with green tips that can be placed in the new pot. Place the bottom of the plant into the new pot, which should be tall enough for the roots to grow into.

Vandas have extensive aerial roots, which will grab and grow on anything.

Using either large pieces of bark or sphagnum moss, fill the pot so the vanda is centered. Vandas are tall, top-heavy plants, so to keep them erect in the pot, use a bamboo plant stake and insert it about ½ inch from the stem of the plant. Use floral wire or raffia to attach the stem to the stake and secure the plant in the pot so the stem doesn't wobble. Water after repotting and make sure that the large bark is not blocking the drainage holes.

✤ TIPS FOR REBLOOMING

Vandas will bloom at least once a year; if yours seems reluctant to do so, move the plant to a location where it will receive more light and sun. That should do the trick.

Dendrobium

The standard dendrobium is a leading plant in the modern cut-flower market.

The genus *Dendrobium* is one of the largest groups of orchids and has probably the most varied plant forms within it. These plants can grow in cool, intermediate, and warm climates, so it is important to know which kind of dendrobium you have, whether the warm-growing tropical type or the cool-growing Australian type.

Dendrobiums are the beautiful mainstay of the cut-flower market; their stems and flowers can last for months. When I first visited Hawaii in the late sixties and disembarked on the tarmac on the runway, I was given my first dendrobium flower orchid lei. Let's just say it was love at first sight.

The name of this incredibly varied genus comes from the Greek word *dendros*, which means "tree," and *bios*, which means "life," as they originally appeared to grow only on trees. With close to a thousand species growing in the region from India through China, Southeast Asia, Japan, Malaysia, the Pacific Islands, and New Zealand and down to Australia, dendrobiums grow in a multitude of forms and sizes, from hardly an inch in size to well over 10 feet tall.

PHALAENOPSIS–TYPE DENDROBIUM

The most common type of dendrobium in the marketplace is confusingly called the phalaenopsis–type dendrobium. This is because the dendrobium flower is slightly similar to the phalaenopsis flower. This is the type that is generally grown for the cut-flower trade. Grown by the millions in Hawaii and other tropical zones around the world, they have been bred to be tough, easy-to-bloom orchids that will blossom when there is no new growth or even leaves on the plant. Phalaenopsis-type dendrobiums are one of the most widely sold plants and every decorator's dream, as these elegant, hardy plants with long-lasting flowers are perfect for interiors. Besides the classic white and pink, they can now be found in yellow and green.

See the similarity in appearance to the phalaenopsis flower? Dendrobiums have an astounding array of growth habits.

Dendrobium kingianum from Australia. This dendrobium also grows well when mounted in tree ferns.

❖ GROWING CONDITIONS

During the most recent orchid craze, this orchid, along with the true phalaenopsis, spearheaded the way into the big-box and supermarket plant departments. This orchid is very easy to grow and rebloom in a house if given good light.

When you get your phal-type dendrobium home, select a very bright location that receives a lot of filtered sunlight. A good tip for this type of orchid is to use a plant tag to keep track of the plant's position and sun orientation (see page 30). This prevents the sun from burning newly exposed foliage and also keeps the direction of the orchid's growth uniform.

❖ WATERING

This type of dendrobium is a little tricky when it comes to watering. The canes (really an elongated pseudobulb that is cane-like in appearance) can become quite large, heavy, and unwieldy, making the simple watering-by-weight approach impractical. Watering weekly is sufficient for most 4- to 6-inch pots during the dormant period, the time when the plant has no growth and is not flowering. When your dendrobium is growing and flowering, water every three to five days, making sure that it is draining properly.

❖ FERTILIZING

All dendrobiums (except for Australian dendrobiums; see following) should be fertilized year-round every two weeks with a 20-20-20 fertilizer.

❖ REPOTTING

Dendrobiums grow well in ridiculously small pots. You'll see huge two-foot-tall canes coming out of a 4-inch container. I like to keep them in their pots for as long as possible and repot only when new plant growth is emerging. Even then, the new pot should be just slightly larger, allowing for no more then two new canes' growth. Dendrobiums grow well in fine- to medium-size bark mixed with a little perlite, or moss.

To repot, remove and untie the cane(s) from any support stakes. Remove the plant from the pot and examine the root-ball. If it's solid with live roots, you can simply insert it into a slightly larger pot with a layer of potting mix at the bottom to bring the level of the plant to slightly below the rim of the pot. Using the same potting mix, fill in around the plant. If some or all of the roots in the root-ball are dead, cut the dead ones away and repot in the same or a smaller-size pot.

❖ TIPS FOR REBLOOMING

Increasing the light usually gets these guys blooming again. Unfortunately, some orchid producers overfertilize these plants in the nurseries, so they are slow to recover once they're in your home, but after a year they will get back on track blooming regularly.

AUSTRALIAN COOL-GROWING DENDROBIUM

Small-size (2 to 6 inches tall) cool-growing dendrobiums from Australia are beginning to crop up everywhere because of their hardiness (they can grow outside wherever frosts are not too bad) and their ability to multiply. The bulbs bloom in the spring with two to seven sweetly fragrant pink-purple flowers each.

❖ GROWING CONDITIONS

Grow these plants in the coolest, brightest room of your house. Although they are very adaptable and will grow in all temperature ranges, they will bloom more dependently if things are a little cool. They will grow in direct sunlight, but seem to grow a little faster when given just morning or afternoon sun.

❖ WATERING

When they are actively growing with the new growth visible, these plants can dry out quickly, so do not be afraid to give them extra water.

These orchids make baby plants, or "keikis," on the end of the bulbs after they flower. When new roots appear at the base of these baby plants, they can be removed and planted in their own pot. After five years of growing an Australian dendrobium, you will likely have accumulated dozens of new plants.

❖ FERTILIZING

These dendrobiums do not need much fertilizer, so feed year-round every four months with a 20-20-20 fertilizer at 50 percent of the recommended strength.

❖ REPOTTING

Because of its small size and robust root system, this plant is a breeze to repot. Wait until you can see the beginnings of new growth at the bottom sides of the bulbs in the pot, and then remove the plant. Remove any old potting medium with your fingers. These orchids like having a compact root system, so I suggest increasing the pot size by only 1 inch each time you repot.

NEW HYBRIDS

With hybridizers coming up with new colors and types all the time, these Australian cuties are now firmly in the world marketplace. They are readily available with pink, white, and purple flowers. Plants with yellow, green, and multi-colored flowers are also available—they're a bit harder to find, but well worth the search.

❖ TIPS FOR REBLOOMING

I have found that the major cause of an Aussie dendrobium failing to flower when grown in the house is that the buds rot while developing within the sheath. These flowers bloom indoors in late winter or whenever it is cold outside and the household heat is high. The newly developing flowers in the sheath are extremely vulnerable to bud rot, which occurs easily with rapid air temperature changes. In early spring, make sure that this plant is in a location with even air circulation. It might be smart to buy a little fan to avoid any overheating (see page 40).

Cymbidium

This orchid has been grown and revered in China for thousands of years. The name cymbidium is derived from the Greek word *kymbes*, which means "boat-shaped," referring to the lip of the flower. The plants are found in nature in the region from India to Southeast Asia, China, Japan, Indonesia, and Australia.

In the world market, there are three main groups of cymbidiums: standard, modern, and Asian miniature. The standard is the large, common cool-growing cymbidium with large flowers, ideal for growing outside in cool and temperate climates. I grew up with standard cymbidiums in California, where they grow abundantly in gardens and yards, both in the pot and in the ground. They can become huge, which makes

A modern white cymbidium hybrid

them difficult to keep as houseplants, so buy these if you are looking for an outdoor plant and live in a climate that can accommodate them (see "Outdoor Growing Guide," page 54). But anyone who has enough indoor space for them will find them easy to bloom anywhere.

MODERN CYMBIDIUM

A hybrid of the standard cymbidium and the warmer-growing Asian miniature cymbidium, this plant can be grown in both cool climates and warmer areas such as Southern California and Florida. This orchid appeared in the marketplace around 1995. Within the last decade, major California and Florida growers started producing these plants in the tens of thousands. They are tolerant of warm climates, which makes them ideal for growing in the house. The growing tips below apply to the modern cymbidium as well as the standard cymbidiums, the difference being that modern cymbidiums can tolerate warmer temperatures.

ASIAN MINIATURE CYMBIDIUM

What this warm-growing plant lacks in size, it makes up for with incredible fragrance and purity of form. This type of cymbidium is considered so graceful that it has been used in Chinese art for centuries. Hundreds of types are grown in Japan and China, and the rarer forms can come with a hefty price tag. Asian miniature cymbidiums should be grown in warmer (55° to 90°F) temperatures than standard and modern cymbidiums but other than that (and the obvious difference in size), they can be cared for in the same way.

❖ **GROWING CONDITIONS**

Cymbidiums will bloom readily when given good morning or afternoon sun. Exposing the

A group of mini, modern, and standard cymbidiums: note the difference in size.

plant to too much sun, though, will yellow the leaves, so moderate the sun exposure if this starts to happen. Make sure the drainage is always good, as a clogged drainage hole will result in a rotted root system. Cymbidiums grown in the ground outside will need less water and fertilizer than their indoor cousins, as their roots have more water gathering opportunity, and more natural fertilizer is available to them.

If you are growing cymbidiums outside, you must keep the crowns and the base of the plants free from leaf and stem debris. Debris will quickly break down into dirt that can cover and rot new flower spikes and growth. I recommend weekly inspection and cleaning to allow the flower to bloom.

For indoor plants, find a place by a window that gets some sunshine, preferably morning or afternoon sun, but not too close to the glass to avoid burning the leaves. Cymbidium leaves are very susceptible to spider mites in the house, so every time you water be sure to rinse the entire plant, including the underside of the leaves. This practice will keep mites at bay.

I recommend keeping your cymbidiums, like other orchids, well groomed. This makes for a more attractive plant; also, stripping off old leaves and sheaths removes hiding places for bugs.

❖ WATERING

Cymbidiums love water; they have lots of roots and should be watered weekly.

❖ FERTILIZING

These plants are generally heavy feeders. You can use a 20-20-20 fertilizer at the strength recommended by the manufacturer while they are growing leaves and creating bulbs. Once the new bulb has matured, switch to a 0-10-10 blooming fertilizer to encourage blooming. After the plant has finished blooming, switch back to the first fertilizer. If you are growing

your cymbidiums outside, dilute the 20-20-20 fertilizer by two-thirds more than recommended on the package or bottle.

❖ REPOTTING

My advice is to learn how to repot cymbidiums, then find a job that pays well enough that you can hire someone to repot your cymbidiums. This is backbreaking work. When I was younger and looking for extra money, I would travel around the Bay Area repotting cymbidiums for people who didn't have the strength or patience to repot and divide their monstrous plants. They repotted their miniature and modern cymbidiums themselves.

The best time to repot a cymbidium is after it has bloomed and is showing new growth. The saying "Don't repot cymbidiums after the Fourth of July" is true; early July is the cut-off time for repotting. By then, the new growth and new roots are far too developed and the plant does not want to be disturbed. Repotting this late will cause the new growth to stunt, resulting in the absence of flowers the following season.

Removing a cymbidium from its pot is tough. If it is in a clay pot and you want to save the pot, this can take an hour, as you have to wedge a long, dull knife between the pot and the roots and work your way around, usually more than once, until the plant slips out. If all else fails, take a hammer to the pot to break it and release the plant, but be careful of the sharp shards.

If your cymbidium is growing in a large plastic pot and does not come out when you pull on it, lay the pot on its side and, being careful not to hurt the foliage, step on the plant. Rotate the pot 90 degrees and step on the plant again, and repeat until you have stepped on all four sides. If it is still stuck in the pot, get some heavy shears and cut the plastic pot off.

If you are moving a cymbidium to a larger pot, wet the root-ball, removing all loose potting medium and debris, and cut off any dead roots. If there are no dead roots present, you can leave the root-ball as is and move the plant to a larger pot, allowing enough space for two new bulbs of the same size as the present bulbs to grow between the plant and the edge of the pot. Cymbidiums do well in fine bark with perlite mix or moss (although it can be expensive if you need a lot of moss for a large plant).

✤ TIPS FOR REBLOOMING

Standard cymbidiums need a day-night temperature difference of at least 30°F to bloom well, and that is hard to do in a house. Modern and Asian cymbidiums need a 25°F difference. So, if the weather is good and you can achieve the required temperature fluctuation by putting a plant outside at night and bringing it in during the day for a few days, do so.

If you are growing your cymbidium outside, make sure you constantly remove all fallen leaves and debris that accumulate on the orchid and in the pot. If not cleaned out, this material will decompose and cover your emerging flower spikes and rot them out. Snails and slugs love cymbidium flowers and spikes and can eat them before you ever see them.

Cymbidiums respond very well to blooming fertilizers. Just follow the instructions on the package and you should be good to go. Generally, you can start to apply fertilizer after the new bulb is the same size as the other bulbs in the pot.

Reed-Stem Epidendrum

Reed-stem epidendrum. The flower spike should not be cut unless the spike is totally brown and dried and dead. New flowers and keikis will continue to emerge from the spike after the primary blooming.

These plants get their name from the Greek words *epi*, which means "upon," and *dendron*, which means "tree," for when first discovered, that's where they were growing. In nature, they range from Mexico to South America and are one of the easiest orchids to grow. They adapt readily to almost any environment, both indoors and outdoors. The flowers are small and cluster at the ends of the stems, making little flower heads, which on a mature plant can bloom for three months or more. The color variety is wide, with orange and red being the most popular and whites, yellows, pinks, and purples available as well. Outdoor plants attract hummingbirds, which is a delightful bonus.

✤ GROWING CONDITIONS

Epidendrums growing in the house prefer morning or afternoon sun in a very bright room. Grow them as close to the window as you can without yellowing the leaves (the plants will reach for the sunlight so make sure that they do not touch the glass). Although these orchids certainly love the sun, I have found that in the house where it is dry and air circulation poor, they can burn easily, so just be mindful. In areas of severe winters, even a double paned window will not prevent your epidendrum from damage from the cold if it touches the glass.

All orchids love fresh air, but this orchid especially does. Just placing the pot outside in the warmer months will result in noticeably increased growth and vigor for your epidendrum. If the plant has never had direct sun exposure, place it in a location in the shade. As the plant acclimates, increase the level of direct sunshine slowly.

✤ FLOWER BEDS

Growing epidendrums in flower beds in the ground is possible anywhere where cymbidiums and Australian dendrobiums are grown. A bed of these brightly colored orchids is visually impressive and mature beds will flower almost year round. Spring is the best time of year to start your bed of epidendrums just as new roots are starting to break on the plants.

✤ KEIKIS ("BABY ORCHIDS")

Epidendrums grow baby orchids (keikis) from both the old canes and flower spikes, so do not cut off the old canes or flower spikes unless they are completely brown, withered, and dead. These little keikis will make roots. When they have made three new little roots, you remove them by holding the base of the keiki and snapping them off. These baby plants can then be potted by themselves, or placed back into the pot or bed in empty areas. If there are a lot of canes on the plant, you can also break

Beds of reed-stem epidendrums in a backyard in Florida.

off large pieces containing at least seven leaves or nodes and replant them bottom side down, three nodes deep, where they will readily root and send off new growth. This is a good way to increase the pot or bed size. A large pot of epidendrums can be divided into dozens of plants.

✤ WATERING

Watering the entire plant once a week generally works well for epidendrums. Once the plant is showing new leaves and roots, watering should be increased to once every three to five days to ensure that the plant doesn't dry out.

✤ FERTILIZING

Fertilize your epidendrum every two weeks year-round, using a 20-20-20 fertilizer. If grown outside in beds, once a month is fine.

✤ REPOTTING

The best time to repot epidendrums is in the early summer when new growth and roots appear at the base of the plant. The new growth should be about 1 inch tall, just making its first leaf. Water the plant before beginning. Remove the plant from its pot and remove the old potting medium. This orchid has a rambling, climbing growth habit, and the majority of the dead growth will be found below the level of the potting medium. Cut away all the dead growth, and then bury the good roots in the medium, using either a fine-to-medium-size bark and perlite mix or just straight sphagnum moss. Water the plant again after repotting and check that it's draining well.

Epidendrums also produce baby plants on their flower spikes after the plant has bloomed. These little plants, or keikis, will make roots. When they have made at least three roots, remove the baby from the old spike by snapping it off with your hand. You can then plant it back in the pot, or put it in its own new pot.

✤ TIPS FOR REBLOOMING

These plants will continue to bloom on the same flower spike for over a year. When the

NEW REED-STEM EPIDENDRUM HYBRIDS

Because of their growing popularity and great flower presentation, new hybrids of epidendrums are constantly being produced. However, when crossed with orchids such as cattleya, a warmer environment is required. Since epi-catt hybrids look identical to regular epidendrums, be sure to check the tag or ask the vendor if the plant can be grown outside in your area.

plant appears to have finished blooming, cut off about 1 inch of the spike from the top of the plant, and a new flower spike will start to grow from the old spike. If the end of the spike is already dead, follow the spike downwards with your eyes and find the spot where the stem is no longer brown. Cut off the dead spike about an inch below where the green healthy part of the stem starts, and a new flower spike will appear.

AMERICA'S EPIDENDRUM EPIPHYTE: *EPIDENDRUM MAGNOLIAE*

Many years ago, I was invited to go canoeing on the Suwannee River. My hostess told me that the Greenfly orchid *Epidendrum conopseum* (now called *Epidendrum magnoliae*) could be found growing on the old oak trees on the banks. Minutes into the trip, I found these plants and was completely blown away. Colonies in full bloom were growing in moss on the branches that stretched over the water. When we returned that evening and it was getting dark, I could smell their fragrance in the air.

You can find these magnificent orchids growing as far north as North Carolina and on the Gulf Coast as far west as Louisiana.

A yellow masdevallia hybrid

These orchids are the jewels of the cool-growing (40° to 80°F) orchid world. The colors of masdevallias are incredibly bright and vibrant. In the past twenty years, this orchid has exploded in popularity in the market, with many growers breeding them to be more heat resistant. The masdevallia was named in honor of a famous eighteenth-century Spanish botanist, Dr. José Masdevall. It does well in the cool parts of a house and grows very well outdoors in hardiness zones 8, 9, and 10 (see "Outdoor Growing Guide," page 54).

✤ GROWING CONDITIONS

Masdevallias should be grown in a semi shady location in a cool room with good air circulation. Usually, the coolest room in the house faces north and is on the bottom floor, so try there first. In my greenhouse, I prefer to grow these plants in sphagnum moss in clay pots,

taking care to water them frequently. But in homes where they are watered once a week, it is best to grow them in plastic pots using a fine bark mixed with small-size perlite.

✤ WATERING

Masdevallias should be watered frequently enough so that they never get dry. They like to be moist. You must check them often during periods of warm weather, as they can dry out surprisingly fast. When growing in low-humidity areas, water the entire plant to keep mites at bay. You can water them slightly less during late winter, when daylight is shorter and the pots take longer to dry out.

✤ FERTILIZING

I suggest using a 10-10-10 fertilizer diluted by 50 percent more than the recommended dose every 2 weeks. Masdevallias collect excess salts easily and their new roots are particularly sensitive, so watch for salt buildup on leaves.

✤ REPOTTING

Repot your masdevallia whenever it is loose in its pot, as this indicates that the root system has broken down and is no longer supporting the plant. It should also be repotted if the mix is soggy or smells foul or sour, as this indicates that the plant has been overwatered or its drainage is impaired. My current favorite potting medium to use is sphagnum moss, as I have found that it helps to keep the roots cool and allows them to grow more vigorously, but if you can water only once a week, use fine bark mixed with small-size perlite. Water the plant before starting. Remove the plant from its pot and wash away the old mix. Cut off and remove the old roots, especially any dead roots in the middle of the root-ball. If using moss, fill the cavity where you removed roots from the root-ball with moss and then

Masdevallia species and hybrids—note the astonishing color variety.

wrap new moss around the outside of the root-ball, using just enough so that you can slip the root-ball back into a slightly larger pot. Masdevallias like being grown in a relatively small pot, so leave just a little room between the plant and the new pot.

✤ **TIPS FOR REBLOOMING**

Increasing air circulation will sometimes help these flowers to bloom. Masdevallia flower spikes emerge from the base of their solitary leaf, and the sheath that covers the spike is very small and prone to either rotting or drying out before the flower spike can. Increasing the air movement in the room helps to correct both conditions.

If you live in a warm region and the plant is otherwise growing well, try sticking it in the vegetable bin of your refrigerator for a few nights to give it a good cool-down. Just be sure to remember to take it out every morning.

WARM-GROWING MASDEVALLIAS

Although masdevallias are generally known as cool growers, there are some species and new hybrids that are easy to grow in a warm house:

Masdevallia Angel Tang
Masdevallia erinacea
Masdevallia goliath
Masdevallia infracta
Masdevallia Ken Dole
Masdevallia Maui Jewell
Masdevallia nidifica
Masdevallia pygmaea
Masdevallia rex
Masdevallia Snowbird
Masdevallia tonduzii
Masdevallia tovarensis
Masdevallia tubuliflora

A GREAT OLD ORCHID

The first records of masdevallias appeared in the late 1770s, written by Spanish botanists, and by Victorian times masdevallias were firmly entrenched in the orchid scene. In the 1980s, I was living in San Francisco, a masdevallia growers' hub, and suddenly I was awash with new and rediscovered *Masdevallia* species that seemed to appear monthly as roads and infrastructures were built in the central and South American jungles. Over twenty years ago, I crossed *Masdevallia coccinea* with *Masdevallia triangularis* and came up with some great plants. However, my exuberance was short lived when I found out that the cross had already been made over a hundred years ago!

Vanilla Orchid

Revered from pre-Columbian times, the legendary vanilla orchid is steeped in intrigue. It still surprises me that most people do not realize that the vanilla plant is an orchid. The "vanilla bean" is this orchid's seed pod. *Vanilla* is a Spanish word meaning "long pod," referring to the seed pod. Vanillas are widely cultivated around the world (including Arizona!) for their pods, which are dried and used whole in cooking or to make vanilla extract. There are many species and types of vanilla orchids, which has led to an appreciation of the variations in the flavor of their pods. Vanilla plants are commonly offered at orchid society sales and shows and through orchid magazines, and are quickly becoming easier to find in the standard orchid market.

✤ GROWING CONDITIONS

The vanilla orchid grows and looks like a vine rather than the usual orchid plant. It is one of the very few monopodial terrestrial orchids

A vanilla orchid in flower

and is very easy to grow in the house, in temperatures ranging from 60° to 80°F. This plant likes shade, so if you are growing it on a window ledge, you should let it climb up around the window where it is not directly in the sun's path. The persistent roots will grow and attach themselves directly to the wood of the sill, or wrap themselves around any stake for support. The roots like being supported—in nature they climb up trees—so try using a stick of tree fern in the pot. Popular belief is that the vine has to be at least 6 feet long before you can expect flowers, but I have seen vanillas blooming on vines less than 2 feet tall. All vanilla species have green and white flowers that are 1 to 3 inches in size, are very fragrant, and live for only a day.

✤ WATERING

Remember that the vanilla is a climbing vine, so it is just as important to water the new roots that emerge from the stem at the top of the plant as it is to water the plant itself. The roots on vanilla plants that are closer to the ground grow robustly downward when they enter the potting medium. The roots on the upper part of the vine grow outward and are designed for supporting the vine's upward growth; they respond quickly when they are given something to grab. Vanillas like a regular watering schedule and as much humidity as you can give them, making them an ideal choice for a kitchen window over the sink.

✤ FERTILIZING

Due to the vine-like growth of these orchids, watering and fertilizing can be a bit tricky. Be sure to fertilize any roots that appear on the vine and leaf nodes, as well as the roots in the pot. The roots grow quickly and will adhere to almost any surface, including walls, so unless

A single vanilla flower

you are planning to grow the plant there forever, train the roots to follow the vine down into the pot by tying them to the vine. This will make fertilizing easier. Use a 10-10-10 fertilizer as directed, year-round.

✤ REPOTTING

The base of a vanilla plant tends to rot if the potting medium becomes the least bit stale or muddy looking, indicating that the bark has broken down and the roots are rotting. When new roots coming down from the upper vine avoid entering the pot and run over rather than enter the potting medium, you'll know you have a problem. Be sure to check the base of the plant occasionally. If rot does occur, the base of the plant will turn brown or black and feel mushy. When this happens, cut the vine off about one inch above the rotted base, discard the base, and make sure you clean and wash the old pot before you use it again. Plant the vine in a new pot with great drainage, in a mix of four parts clean fine bark and one part medium- or large-size perlite. Tree fern stakes can be used for support, as the roots will quickly grow into the tree fern, allowing the roots more moisture and adding stability. As the vine grows, which it does rather quickly when healthy, you can train it to frame the window.

✤ TIPS FOR REBLOOMING

The old myth that a vanilla vine has to be 6 feet long before you can expect a flower is just a myth. I have seen vanilla plants blooming that were less than a foot tall. I think blooming for this flower mostly has to do with an established root system, so make sure the roots that descend from the vine are getting into the pot or being sufficiently nourished if grown on a treefern slab. If all of the roots seem healthy and alive, try treating the plant with a blooming fertilizer in late fall.

GROWING A VANILLA BEAN

To grow your own vanilla bean, check your vanilla orchid for flowers, which will appear at the nodes of the leaves. When these flowers open, they last for only a day. You must pollinate a flower in order to grow a bean. To do this, locate the flower column (where all the reproductive organs are), which is just above the lip. The pollen is concealed at the end of the flower column in a little cap. Look underneath the cap and you will see a little white flap hanging down. Brush the end of a toothpick toward you against the little flap; the flap will stick to the toothpick and you will pull out the yellow pollen attached to the flap. You will see a little cavity behind the hole where the pollen was. Place the pollen in the cavity, which is called the stigmatic cavity, and the pollen will stick to it. Leave it there and the magic will start. The ovary, which is at the end of the stem behind the flower, will send out tubes, and after a few days, a green seedpod will start to form. After a few months, it will plump up and turn green. It takes about nine months for the bean to mature. It will start to lose its green color, and you should pick it before it turns completely yellow. Let the pod dry in the sun or in an oven with a pilot light for a few days before using.

A miniature pleurothallis orchid

There is a whole other orchid world out there: mini orchids (including those already discussed; see page 89). These little jewels deserve their own section because they are so lovely and are becoming more common every day. Their small size allows for a greater diversity of species to be grown in the house, and orchid hybridizers are racing to create new types. They are highly sought after in metropolitan areas like New York and Chicago, where space is minimal.

In addition to the benefits that come from their smaller size, there are other advantages to miniature orchids: supplies cost less, pests and other problems are easier to spot, repotting is simple, and it is easier to regulate their climate. For example, if an orchid is dehydrated, you can make a mini greenhouse by simply covering the plant with a clear plastic container.

The variety of miniature orchids is endless, and all of the major orchid types have a miniature form. There are miniature oncidiums with dime-size bulbs that produce 10-inch spikes of little dancing yellow flowers, for example. There's a miniature phalaenopsis one-fifth the size of the regular-size plant, and miniature cymbidiums have flowers one-tenth the size of a standard cymbidium. My favorite mini belongs to genus Dendrobium, *Dendrobium cuthbersonii*; the flower spikes are just ½ inch tall and produce stunningly crystalline, fiery 1-inch red or orange flowers that last for two months. There are hundreds of miniature orchids out there just waiting to sweep you down the river of orchid love!

✤ **GROWING CONDITIONS**

The only drawback to entering the world of minis is that their diminutive size requires increased maintenance and care, as their small pots can dry out daily in warm weather or when the heat in the home is on consistently.

Miniature orchids have the same growing needs as standard orchids, but generally thrive with a little less light. Do not grow them close to a south-facing window with sun, as they can fry in hours. Early-morning or late-afternoon sun is best, with the plants kept away from the window glass. I have seen all types growing well in a bright north-facing window, where they also retain a little more moisture.

✤ **FERTILIZING**

These little plants need their food, but because of their tiny roots, you have to be careful not to overfertilize. Always use a 10-10-10 mix, diluting the recommended dosage by 50 percent. Fertilize every two weeks year round. Because of the small-size pots, many people just submerge them in a pail of water for watering, but these plants should not be soaked in fertilizer water for more than a minute at a time because their little roots are tender.

✤ **WATERING**

As I have emphasized, small pots need frequent watering and daily attention. It really helps to grow miniature orchids in your kitchen (being

An incredible range of flower types and colors can be found in miniature orchids.
Note: the smallest pot in this picture is 1 inch, the largest is 3 inches!

mindful of temperature increases while cooking) or bathroom, where water is readily accessible and they can be regularly monitored.

✦ REPOTTING

This is my favorite thing about miniature orchids: I have never strained my back, poked myself in the eye, cut myself, or dropped a pot on my foot when repotting them. The extra time you spend watering is worth it for the ease of repotting an orchid in a 1-inch pot. Though you may have to squint.

Prepare the potting medium according to the size of the roots and plant. When using fine-size bark, clean and examine the bark first, getting rid of any big pieces and cutting other pieces into a uniform size with small scissors; this allows for even drainage in the small pots. When using sphagnum moss, I also suggest cutting it into smaller pieces because it makes it easier to work the moss around the small roots. Just as with standard orchids, you must carefully remove the plant from its pot and gently remove the old mix. Using nail scissors, cut off any dead roots and growth and any damaged or dead flower spikes or leaves. This way, if any future damage or problems occur, you will know it is recent.

You must pay attention to the roots and the level of the plant when repotting. Make sure that the roots are not bent or broken during repotting and that the orchid is not planted too deep or too high in the pot. With the small size of these plants, it is easy to bury the emerging new growth from the base of the plant, so remember that the base of the plant should be on the same level as the potting mix. Water very gently after repotting, and make sure the pot is draining.

✦ TIPS FOR REBLOOMING

With miniatures, we are dealing with a wide variety of orchid types that grow on different schedules, so it's hard to give specific reblooming advice here. But I have found that the most common causes of lack of blooms with these small plants are irregular watering and insufficient light. It is generally recommended to give miniatures low light, but you should increase their light if they do not bloom.

Ten Contenders

In addition to the twelve popular orchid types outlined in this chapter, there are ten more orchids that are quickly gaining prominence in the emerging orchid marketplace. Keep an eye out for these special plants in the coming years.

ANGRAECUM

Angraecums and their new hybrids are easy to spot because of their forest green fan-shaped leaves and their large, pristine white flowers with a long spur hanging down. These orchids have an enchanting nighttime fragrance that adds to the plant's popularity.

MILTONIA

Twenty years ago this genus of warm-growing orchids from Brazil also contained what is now the genus *Miltoniopsis*, which is from Costa Rica and the Andes and is cool growing. They are now split into two separate genera. An easy way to tell them apart is that miltonias have two-leafed bulbs (really pseudobulbs), while miltoniopsis have one-leafed bulbs. Two of these warm-growing orchids, *Miltonia spectabilis* and *Miltonia regnellii*, have flowers that look like pansies, but the plants are larger and the bulbs not as clustered; the other miltonias look like large brown oncidiums. This group has been hybridized heavily with oncidiums and other related types to produce heat-tolerant, colorful flowers for warmer climates.

ZYGOPETALUM

This cool- to moderate-temperature-growing orchid is now being bred for warmer temperatures. Zygopetalums are gaining in popularity due to their strong growth habit and fragrant purple flowers.

SOBRALIA

A stately orchid that looks and grows just like bamboo, with flowers that resemble cattleyas. It produces one of the largest flowers in the orchid world, and is being developed to grow in both cool and warm climates.

DENDROCHILUM

An elegant warm-growing orchid with grass-like foliage and delightfully scented pendant flowers, this one is easy to grow in the home.

BLETILLA

This hardy terrestrial orchid seems able to grow and bloom almost everywhere. Breeding has taken off in recent years, resulting in dozens of new hybrids.

GRAMMATOPHYLLUM

One of the largest orchids, found in the jungle from Indochina to New Guinea, grammatophyllum is being grown and bred in ever-increasing numbers in Hawaii and Florida. Its summer blooming habit helps its marketability, as few other large plants bloom then.

PHAIUS

With a huge natural range from China to Africa, this large, warm-growing orchid has been in cultivation for hundreds of years. It is enjoying a renaissance of breeding efforts, and can be found growing abundantly in nature in Hawaii.

NEOFINETIA

This famous "wind," or "samurai" orchid from Japan, with its covetable small size, grace, and

Angraecum veitchii. This orchid has a very strong nocturnal fragrance.

Bletilla striata can be grown indoors, and outdoors nearly anywhere.

fragrance, will soon be available the world over as growers rapidly propagate and breed it.

PSYCHOPSIS

Known as the "butterfly orchid," psychopsis is said to have started the Victorian orchid craze and understandably so. The flower appears at the end of a long, thin flower spike that disappears from a distance, so that the flower looks like a huge gold and brown butterfly in flight. There are few flowers in the world that are as exotic-looking, and the leaves of this orchid are attractive as well, with beautiful reddish spotted leaves. We can look forward to seeing more of these plants in the marketplace.

THE MOST AMUSING ORCHIDS

CATASETUMS / This orchid from Central and South America is pretty unique. It shoots—and I mean shoots—out pollen when it senses a trigger, such as the antennae of an insect. It releases the pollen with great force in order to attach it to its pollinator, and, in the absence of a bee, the pollen will shoot a couple of feet! This orchid is great at parties.

CORYANTHES / Also from Central and South America, these orchids have huge flowers with a lip that folds into a bucket shape. The column above the lip actually drips a watery honey-tasting fluid directly into the flower. It's wild!

OPHRYS / These orchids can be found in the range from Europe to Western Asia and the flowers look exactly like bees (meant, of course, to attract bees). They don't just resemble bees—they look like actual bees!

BULBOPHYLLUM MEDUSAE / This smaller orchid's flower has thin, stringy petals that hang down like hair. They almost look like little friendly monsters rather than orchids.

A yellow phalaenopsis hybrid. Just twenty years ago, this was one of the most expensive and hardest hybrids to find; now it is common.

Part Four

DECORATING
WITH ORCHIDS

From long-lasting flowers to elegant presentation, the advantages of decorating with orchids are many. You can find orchids small enough to fit in a thimble or large enough to fill a 6-foot urn; you can match nearly any color of the rainbow. Orchids are also an economical décor choice. With today's distribution of bloomers like phalaenopsis and dendrobiums, you can purchase a nice orchid for twenty dollars and enjoy its blooms for a month or more. Amazingly, some cut orchids can also last up to a month, much longer than your average cut flowers such as tulips or roses.

I have been decorating with orchids for over twenty-five years. Sometimes people compliment me on my talent, which feels good (especially if my wife is around). Truth be told, my talent is more a result of experience and experimentation than anything else. Decorating with orchids is trial and error, and you'll get better the more you do it. Play around at first—place your orchid in different locations, in different containers, and in different lighting situations, to see which ones work for you.

Start by thinking about what a specific orchid could add to a particular space. For instance, for a demure or conservatively themed bedroom, I would select species with proper-looking flowers, such as *Brassivola nodosa* or *Epidendrum parkinsonianum*, to echo the feel of the room. (Plus, I know that as soon as the lights go out, that room will explode with fragrance—something else to keep in mind while you're decorating.) A Victorian-styled library calls for a classic cattleya or a paphiopedilum in an antique wooden container. A modern reed-stem epidendrum, with its stark, linear foliage and pom-pom-like flowers, although a beautiful orchid, would be as out of place here as an Eames chair.

Setting the Stage

If you are displaying just one orchid in a room, the natural choice of location is the main focal point, such as an entrance table or fireplace mantel. Yet

The phalaenopsis is a beautiful and graceful choice for décor.

orchids also work beautifully as a discreet accent in locations like bathrooms or bedside tables. When choosing the location, first make sure the orchid will be safe there (see page 26).

When buying for a specific location, first consider the entire design and size of the room. Is it a huge entrance hall with 20-foot ceilings that calls for a 6-foot-tall willowy orchid? Or is it a fifties ranch house with lower ceilings, where a shorter, fuller orchid would work better? What will be behind the orchid? If a painting, you will want to frame it with the plant, not hide it. If a blank wall, factor in the color. A pure white phalaenopsis loses its drama against a pure white wall, whereas a richly colored orchid against a white backdrop will command attention.

LIGHTING

When positioning your orchid, always consider the lighting. All orchids are spectacular when lit. Some look better when backlit, and some when lit from the front or the sides. Dark or brightly colored flowers need to be lit from the front or side, as backlighting them causes the color to

AN ILLUMINATING TRICK: READING LIGHTS

Reading lights meant for attaching to books with their little spring clamps work surprisingly well to light an orchid. I prefer the lights with a moveable base that allows you to adjust the light direction once clamped onto the plant or container. These are perfect in locations with no light source, such as tucked-away shelves and corners: they are easily concealed, and the battery life will see you through several parties.

Ten flowers can appear as dozens when placed in front of a mirror.

disappear. For white and thin-textured flowers, I like to light from behind the pot with the light beam facing upward, which gives a very clean look and has the extra effect of the shadows cast by the flowers. A concern here, of course, especially with high-wattage lighting, is the heat emitting from the light source. Intense heat or light cut down on the life of the flower and should be carefully assessed during the placement process.

Battery-powered lights make it possible to add lighting anywhere. I have been using a little battery-powered diode bulb light on a swivel base that I bought at the drugstore for just a few dollars. It easily fits inside or behind an orchid pot, and the beam size can be adjusted from a spot to a floodlight. The great thing about these mini lights is there is no heat factor to worry about. The little lights that look like votive candles are great to use, especially in centerpieces, and can be placed close to the flowers without causing harm.

While lighting your orchid, be sure to check your work from the area you know it will be viewed from. For example, if the display is for a gathering in a dim living room, check your work from where your guests will be sitting. While working, step away and view every time you make an adjustment. You do not need tons of light to highlight an orchid display; it is more about how the light falls on the orchid flowers. If you have a floodlight focused on a hallway table, even moving the orchid a few inches will alter the flowers' color intensity, so experiment.

DECORATIVE CONTAINERS

Choosing the right decorative container for your orchid takes some thought. If your room is decorated in a certain style, the container should reflect that style—an orchid in a brown woven basket is out of place in a sleek stainless-steel kitchen.

I choose only containers that are strong enough stylistically to stand by themselves and be displayed with nothing in them. That is a good test to use when selecting a container. The quality of the container should always match the quality of the décor and never cheapen or detract from the overall presentation of the orchid.

There are endless possibilities for creative containers and displays. This is where you can have fun and bring some personality to the display. I find containers just about everywhere. Once you start looking for containers for your orchids, you'll realize how many options there are.

The best container may be one you already have. If you plan to keep orchids in the dining room, and if it matches your look, Grandma's old soup tureen could be the answer. It will certainly mean more and make a stronger statement than a mass-produced basket from your local import store. Try cleaning up that old wooden box with the missing lid. Go through the attic, basement, and garage. Look for anything interesting that can hold an orchid pot. I've also had luck finding unique containers at antiques stores, garage sales, flea markets, and auctions.

Cachepots, or decorative pots without a drainage hole, are made to display potted plants (and orchids), and you can find them in any historical style and color to match your interior. The styles and shapes are endless within each design style, so shop around as you are bound to find one that is perfect for your space. Antique cachepots are beautiful but expensive; some are lined with copper or leaded tin. My personal favorites are French porcelain ones, with the English wooden types a second favorite.

When selecting a cachepot or any other container for your potted orchid, note and measure the diameter of the opening, as you want to be sure it will fit your orchid pot. Remember that if you grow in clay pots you will need an opening at least 1 inch larger than the size of the pot you wish to display; for example a 4-inch clay pot realistically needs a 5-inch opening to fit, as the outside diameter of a clay pot is almost always greater than the stated size.

Prepping Your Orchid for Display

A yellow leaf, a sloppy finish, an unattractive flower support—any of these things can detract from your presentation and impressive blooms. Pay close attention to the small details as you prepare your orchid for display.

GROOMING

It's important to groom your orchid before putting it on display. If you go early to an orchid show, you will notice some intense plant grooming going on, just as at a dog show. Before exposing a plant to scrutiny, you should make sure it is in pristine condition, especially when it is displayed in your house.

Grooming is best done before the plant is in the decorative container. I usually start with clean scissors, cutting out any dead sheaths, leaves, rotted bulbs, and other debris. If the leaves are spotted or have a fertilizer residue, they should be cleaned. Wash the leaf gently with warm water with a little dish soap. If the residue persists, use a cloth dipped in 70 percent rubbing alcohol and clean again. (This is basically what all the leaf-cleaning and leaf-shine products are composed of, but without the extra weird chemicals.) If this doesn't clean it, you might need to cut off the damaged leaf.

LINING YOUR CONTAINER

Make sure that your container is watertight. Just a little spilled or leaking water can cause expensive damage to a wooden tabletop or antique inlaid table. The fact that orchids are grown in porous potting media makes them prone to leakage, so it pays to be extra careful when lining your containers.

I recommend using more than just the shallow plastic trays that are sold to line containers (they often crack or collapse under the pot). Add two or three stacked plastic bag liners as well. Or, even better, use heavy-gauge plastic bags like freezer bags, bringing the sides of the bag all the way up to the top of the inside of the container and securing it with double-sided tape. I usually use two to be safe.

Next, fill any empty space in the container with moss or crumpled paper towels or paper bags (avoid newspaper, because it can smell bad when moist) so that the pot fits snugly. If the container to be used is exceptionally deep, after lining it with plastic bags, you can use an inverted pot or coffee or soup can to raise the inside level and to provide ballast if the container is too heavy. The orchid pot should not be sunken in the container, nor should the top of the pot extend beyond the top of the container. Remember, you want to have easy access to the plant for watering. You'll need to remove the orchid to water it, then allow it to drain as much as possible before returning it to the decorative container, so you don't want to have to completely redo your arrangement every week.

FLOWER AND STEM SUPPORT

Before placing the orchid in the container, think about flower and stem support. That green or metal stick that came with the plant is there to best support and show off the flowers, but it can be ugly and distracting. Replace the support if you don't like it, but do so carefully.

First, untie or cut the wire or remove the orchid clips attaching the spike to the old stake. If the spike is floppy, attach it to a temporary stake with an orchid clip to keep it from breaking. Take out the old stake slowly, being careful not to harm the flowers. If the placement is correct, use the old hole for the new stake. Tie raffia around both the new stake and spike, or use your orchid clips.

Select a support that will not overwhelm the flowers and that blends with the décor of the room. There are many ornamental branches and types of sticks and bamboo available from florists, crafts shops, and garden centers:

❖ *Curly willow branches* / Willow branches are ideal for decorating. The main stalks are strong and not too wide, and the smaller branches twist and curl, providing great support for flower spikes and creating visual intrigue. The branches can be trimmed to achieve a less ornate look. Use twist ties colored to match the color of the branch or raffia for tying.

❖ *Natural bamboo* / Bamboo blends in nicely with the plant and is ideal for Pacific Rim styles. Lacquered bamboo looks especially nice and is widely available. Use raffia for tying.

❖ *Plexiglas rods* / Plexiglas is easy to find in a variety of lengths and widths, and works well in modern decor. Use fishing line for tying.

❖ *Brass and copper rods and tubing* / These supports can be found in hobby, hardware, and crafts stores. Brass works in traditional settings and copper in modern interiors. Use brass or copper wire for tying.

❖ *Nothing!* I always remove the orchid stem from the flower stake after buying to see if it supports itself, which many types do, especially paphiopedilums. This approach allows for the most natural presentation.

FINISHING TOUCHES

You don't want the top of the plastic or clay pot exposed in your decorative container. To complete the look, add a finish of some sort. Green moss is a nice natural finish that works with all styles and décor. Add your finish after putting the plant in the chosen container and securing all of your supports. In today's floral marketplaces there are a variety of finishing products to choose from, plus you may have your own growing outdoors in pots or corners of the garden:

❖ *Live moss* / My favorite finishing material is live moss. I like it so much that I grow moss in my greenhouse just for finishing. Look and see if you have some growing around your house. It lifts off surfaces easily; just peel it up. Never

The use of mood moss and intended absence of support sticks give this orchid a natural presentation.

take it all, but rather try to harvest it in strips so you will always have a supply.

QUICK CONTAINERS

If you don't have time to shop for a nice container before an event, these three creative container ideas can work well in a pinch.

FABRIC CONTAINERS / Hide the pot with a lightly starched napkin or piece of fabric. Simply wrap the napkin around the pot (place the pot in a plastic bag to avoid leakage) and tie it closed with a nice ribbon. Secure the fabric to the pot with a hot-glue gun, or use double-sided tape.

SHEET MOSS CONTAINERS / Another creative way to cover an unsightly pot is to wrap it with sheet moss. Cover the pot with a green moss and secure it by tying it with raffia, either finishing it with bows or cutting close to the tie for a cleaner look.

LEAF CONTAINERS / For a simple solution, cover the pot with big, beautiful leaves from your outdoor trees or large leafed shrubs. The bigger the leaf the easier the assembly, so think maple (great in the fall), fig, canna, or banana leaves. Select only flawless leaves to use. Wrap the pot with double-sided tape or use a white glue and, starting from the bottom, flatten the leaves against the pot. On your last row at the top, extend the leaves over the rim so they can be folded back into the pot to hide the potting medium. You can also use raffia and tie the leaves down; this will take up to three pieces of raffia, and the tie-downs should be equally dispersed on the pot. I have done this many times over the years. It is a quick solution that looks well thought out.

❖ *Mood moss* / I am not sure why this type of moss was named mood moss, but I think it is either because the beautiful finish it provides puts you in a good mood, or the high price of this product puts you in a bad mood. This natural green moss comes in medium- and small-size chunky pieces. It is available at most nurseries and garden and plant supply stores. The texture is dense and compact. I usually do not wet this moss, removing it before watering, because it lasts longer when dry. My preferred way to apply it is by carefully fitting the pieces together like a jigsaw puzzle to make it look like one continuous piece of moss.

❖ *Sheet moss* / This green moss is sold in little sheets, either rolled up or layered. The great thing about sheet moss is that you can cut the sheets to fit your container exactly. Just cut a slit in the middle, cut out a hole to fit the base of the plant, and simply slip it around the base of the plant.

❖ *Net-backed moss* / There are several makers of moss glued to a backing of fine plastic netting, generally sold in rolls 1 to 2 feet wide and 4 to 6 feet long. The quality of this moss, usually found in crafts stores, differs greatly, and it doesn't tend to hold up over time and can look pretty fake, as sometimes the shade of green used for coloring looks completely unnatural. The good news is that it is really easy to use: just trim it to fit any container. It is especially handy for finishing large containers.

❖ *Spanish moss* / Spanish moss is readily available at florists and florist supply and crafts shops. It has been treated to eradicate any bugs and pests that naturally inhabit it. This type of moss lasts longest and is widely used, as the gray color and density works well in most settings. This moss is somewhat curly and springy and I sometimes manicure the moss with scissors to calm the visual wildness.

* *Reindeer moss* / This moss (which is actually a lichen) can be found at florists and crafts shops, and it comes in a very pleasing lime green as well as beautiful shades of rust and brown. The major drawbacks to reindeer moss are that some have an unpleasant smell, especially when wet, and those that are dyed or painted can stain things easily when wet.

* *Rock* / Between garden centers and dish aquarium stores, you can find rocks of every color and shape for creative presentations. Try using rocks that match the color of the container or flower. Black rock also works well for a variety of styles and has a sleek effect.

* *Shells* / The colors, sizes, and shapes of shells are endless, and they add a natural feel to any display. With flat bivalve shells, I like to overlap the pieces and create a pattern. Mother-of-pearl shells and fragments are elegant and luminous.

A FINISHING TIP

When using rocks or other finishes, you may have unsightly gaps between the pieces of material if you don't have enough to solidly cover the potting medium. To eliminate this problem, cut a round piece of cardboard to fit inside the pot, cutting a slit, then a hole for the base of the plant. Paint or color the surface of the cardboard to match the color of rock you are using. Place the cardboard in the pot and use that as the base to lay your rocks on, which fools the eye, keeping the color constant.

Displaying for Your Style

In my career, I have worked in many different styles of homes and interiors, and have found container and finishing combinations that work well for particular looks. Here are some suggestions; feel free to add your own creative touch:

CLASSIC

Stick with tradition here. Go for the classic orchids such as cattleya, masdevallia, and cymbidium.

* *Containers* / Antique wood boxes, letter boxes, malachite boxes; tea caddies; French, English, and Dutch porcelain boxes and bowls; classic decorative urns.

* *Supports* / Dark-stained bamboo, brass rods.

* *Ties* / Brass wire, dark twine.

* *Finish* / Green moss.

ASIAN-INFLUENCED/PACIFIC RIM

In the Asian-influenced style, accessorizing is minimal and colors are basic. Containers are very important. Select those that fall into the visual perimeters you have established with your décor. For example, if you have a modern Pacific Rim interior, with mostly blacks and reds in your color scheme, a blue-and-white Ming container will not fly, even though it is Chinese, but a mandarin-red shellacked round box with its top removed will be perfect even though it was made in Finland. In this kind of setting, I prefer to use orchids with graceful and serene flowers, such as phalaenopsis, paphiopedilum, dendrobium, and oncidium.

* *Containers* / Classic Asian pottery, antique Chinese brush pots; black and red lacquered boxes, letter boxes; antique Japanese hibachis (these often have interior bronze or copper liners, which can be used as containers separately); lacquered woven baskets.

* *Supports* / Natural and glazed bamboo; red and black lacquered bamboo, chopsticks.

Get creative with the containers you choose.

The large single flowers of lycaste make for a regal, minimalist presentation.

- *Tie* / Natural raffia.

- *Finishes* / Green moss, polished black river rocks.

VINTAGE/FLEA MARKET

With vintage style, it doesn't matter if the paint on your container is cracking and peeling, or there is a little rust on the tin soda cracker box you've selected. Imperfections work, so show your creativity.

- *Containers* / Old wood or metal boxes, vintage lunch boxes, hat boxes, pretty gift boxes; vintage cracker and hot cereal containers; old pencil holders.

- *Supports* / Any kind of stake, long wooden spoons, vintage kitchen tools.

- *Ties* / Twine, string.

- *Finishes* / Marbles, old game board pieces, brown moss.

MODERN

Take care to notice surfaces and textures here; keep it simple and clean. Select orchids with a striking form, like reed-stem epidendrums and dendrobiums.

- *Containers* / Stainless-steel and chrome bowls; cups with metallic finishes; clear or black Lucite pots; steel or chrome wastepaper baskets.

- *Supports* / Clear Lucite or plastic rods, stainless-steel or chrome rods; black lacquered bamboo.

- *Ties* / Clear fishing line, black plastic-covered wire, silver ribbon.

- *Finishes* / Green moss, rock.

NATURAL

For a natural look, keep it simple and avoid plastics or man-made materials.

- *Containers* / Old stone mortars, woven baskets, paper or wood boxes and containers.

- *Supports* / Natural bamboo, branches.

- *Ties* / Natural twines, raffia, thin leather strips.

- *Finishes* / Rocks, shells, live moss.

ECLECTIC

This is a fun, whimsical style. Get creative with your containers and finishes—don't hold back.

- *Containers* / Jewel boxes, art boxes; sculptures; glass spice and sugar canisters; mirrored canisters and boxes.

- *Supports* / Curtain rods (I have used these many times, complete with finial, especially with large or tall orchids), drumsticks.

A phalaenopsis in a silver sugar bowl

❖ *Ties* / Ribbons, ornate hair clips, metallic tapes.

❖ *Finishes* / Marbles, game board pieces, anything small and surprising.

COMBINING TWO ORCHIDS IN ONE POT

Sometimes the style of a room calls for a big visual impact, which can be achieved by combining two or more orchids in one container.

1. Do this only with orchids grown in sphagnum moss.

2. When selecting orchids, fit them together as they will appear in the container you're using. To create a fuller look, use plants of different flower height and densities. Take into account which way the flower spikes will be facing; if you are displaying the orchids against a wall, you will want the flower spikes arching outward or to the sides.

3. Water the pots thoroughly and gently remove the plants from their pots, leaving the stakes intact.

4. Remove and pluck away excess moss until both root-balls will fit into the new container.

5. Using the wet moss that you have removed, cover the exposed roots and gaps, as you want the finished root-ball to be round or mimicking the shape of the container used.

6. Align the plants so the desired presentation of the flowers is achieved.

7. Insert the combined root-ball into a sandwich or freezer bag; wrap the bag around the root-ball and fit it into the container.

WHEN IT JUST WON'T FIT: TRANSFERRING TO A SMALLER POT

There are times when a client will hand me a new container with a 5-inch opening, then give me an orchid in a 6-inch pot to put in it. I do what the client wants, and this is how I do it:

1. Use only orchids planted in sphagnum moss or redwood fir. This process does not work as well with orchids planted in bark.

2. Water the orchid pot completely and gently ease the orchid out of the pot, leaving any plant stakes in the pot for now. The wet moss will stay together in the root-ball.

3. Hold the plant over the opening of the container to judge how much moss should be removed.

4. Starting from the sides, start gently picking the moss out of the root-ball equally on all sides until enough has been removed that the orchid will slip easily into the new container. If the container is shallower than the former pot, either cut off the protruding end of the stake, or untie the stake from the stem and lift the stake so it is level with the new shorter depth.

5. Using the pieces of moss you have removed, lay a thin layer of wet moss over any exposed roots, then insert the root-ball in a plastic sandwich bag and wrap the root-ball with it, creating a little plastic pot.

6. Using an additional bag as a liner, slip the orchid into its new home. Add moss and finish the container.

Centerpieces

A successful centerpiece looks fabulous from every location around the table. While you are making your centerpiece, try sitting in each seat to be sure it looks right. The container and arrangement should always be kept low to allow for conversation at the table. Here are some of the best containers for centerpieces:

❖ *Soup tureens and serving dishes* / Choose ones that match the dinnerware you are using.

❖ *Silver serving dishes, platters, cups, and bowls* / Silver looks beautiful for formal dinners. With flat platters, use moss to build the elevation of the "ground," starting from the outside edges, until it is level with the top of the pot in order to conceal it.

❖ *Bread baskets* / French bread baskets lined with linen work well. If there is extra fabric, fold the fabric over to hide the pot, leaving the plant and flowers exposed.

❖ *Asian wooden scoops and rice-measuring boxes* / There are flat-bottomed scoops that fit 4-inch pots and have gorgeous wood tones. The rice-measuring boxes can sometimes be found in nesting sets, which make for a striking display when used in a row.

❖ *Seasonal vegetables* / It sounds crazy, but this is not hard to do and creates a festive atmosphere. Just dig a hole in the top of a large vegetable, like a pumpkin or squash, and fit the pot inside so that it is not visible. Cover the top with the piece you cut away. Use a knife to level the bottom of the vegetable so it doesn't tip.

❖ *Branches and cork bark slabs with flowering orchids* / These make for a natural centerpiece and work particularly well for long tables— place a few in a row, back side down, down the length of the table.

CREATIVE CENTERPIECES

My favorite centerpieces are miniature orchid islands. For this technique, use a flat plate for the base of the island. Cover the plate with moss and place the miniature orchids in the center of the base. Pile the moss to hide the pots, so the orchids appear to be growing out of the moss "island." Add other objects, depending on the theme or style: include a little Buddha statue for a serene effect, or an orchid lei to show off even more flowers.

Cut Orchids

There is a great variety of cut orchid flowers on the market today. The most common ones are dendrobiums, oncidiums, phalaenopsis, and cymbidiums.

Most cut orchids can be displayed out of water for hours and sometimes days and still maintain their freshness. This means that there is endless room for creativity when decorating with cut orchids, using individual flowers or entire flower spikes.

CONTAINERS

Just as with potted plants, the quality of your containers for cut flowers should be on par with your entire presentation or style. If you are displaying for just one night, orchid flowers might not need a container that holds water at all, so let your imagination run wild.

❖ *Liquor or shot glasses* / These tiny glasses are ideal for single large cymbidium or cattleya flowers.

❖ *Soap dishes* / My favorite soap dishes are the shallow crystal ones that are just deep enough to float such small orchid flowers as oncidium.

A single stem in a skinny vase has a striking effect.

✤ *Tiny vases* / These are easy to find, in both glass and pottery, and just the right size for a single phalaenopsis flower.

✤ *Antique salt cellars* / These can be quite elegant, in silver or cut crystal. It is also easy to find matching sets.

✤ *Vases, martini blenders, or water pitchers* / Use these bigger containers for large and long flower spikes. I have even used umbrella stands for massive cut flower spikes such as cymbidiums (which worked very well, as it was an antique made of dark wood and was used in a paneled library).

FLOATING IN WATER

Cut orchid flowers look beautiful floating in water, either individually or as a collection of different types and colors. Use glass bowls and containers of any size and color that fit your décor. Fill with water, add your cut flowers, using colors to match your look, and you have instant décor. I once used an Italian olive pit trough, which was the perfect length and width for a table centerpiece.

GARLANDS

I love to assemble garlands and swags with cut orchid stems. I have used them to accent doorways, cover banisters on stairways, border ceilings, and in every way you can use garlands. Easy-to-find oncidiums and dendrobiums work very well, primarily because the stems are thick with flowers and their long stem length allows for easy assembly. The main thing to consider is whether or not the flowers will last for the length of the event. Some showy orchids, for example miltonias, will collapse quickly after being cut and out of water. Dendrobiums, cymbidiums, phalaenopsis, disas, and oncidiums are the longest-lasting commercially available cut orchid flowers.

Cut orchid stems are sold by the bunch (six stems), or as single stems, in a variety of colors. You can mix colors if you wish. Orchid stems are usually 2 to 3 feet long, with the bottom half stem only, and the top half with the flowers.

The following instructions are for one 3-foot double-stem garland, but you can make garlands as long or as thick as you like, to hang from doorways or wrap around banisters.

✤ **DENDROBIUM ORCHID GARLAND**

What you need:
1. Six cut dendrobium stems
2. Thin green floral wire cut into fifteen 3-inch pieces (cut with strong scissors or a wire cutter)

How to make:
On a table as long as the length of garland you are making, lay two orchid stems side by side with the bare stem ends together. Push the

Floating phalaenopsis flowers will last for weeks.

stems close so that the flowered ends touch, appearing thicker. Repeat with a second pair of stems. Lay the flowered ends of the second pair on top of the bare stems of the first pair to give the effect of continual flowers with no gaps. Repeat with the last two stems.

Starting from the end, make your first tie, using wire to tie the stems together, being careful not to twist the wire so tight that it breaks the stems. Wire as you go, making ties every 4 inches. When you reach the part with two bare stems and two stems with flowers lying together, tie all four of the stems together, making sure that there is no gap in the flowers. It is important to always tie the ends of the stems together, so if the garland is bent, the ends do not pull away from the garland. Continue tying every 4 inches. Cut off the remaining two bare stems after the last tie.

Using more wire, attach the garland to small nails wherever you wish it placed. Cut off any excess wire. Makes one 3-foot garland.

ORCHID LEIS

Orchid leis can be purchased or ordered from your local florist and even from big-box stores. Leis can be used in endless ways, from centerpieces to combining and weaving the leis together to make garlands for bordering mirrors and windows, or to wear. Leis look beautiful tied end-to-end as ropes for weddings or reception lines. To use leis as centerpieces, lay them down the center of the table, or hang them between candlesticks, or coil them on top of each other to make mounds of flowers. One of my favorite things to do with leis is to cut and attach them as needed to create a gorgeous flowered curtain for a doorway.

Decorating with Miniature Orchids

There is a parallel universe of visual delight waiting to be explored: the miniature orchid! I love decorating with these plants. You can find miniature orchids that will fit in a thimble. Take *Dendrobium cuthbertsoniai*, for example: the brilliantly colored flowers, barely an inch long, will last, no exaggeration, for three months. Miniature orchids are ideal for use in bedrooms and bathrooms where you have limited space. There are hundreds of species of these diminutive charmers, and as their popularity grows, dozens of new hybrids are introduced every year (see page 102 for more on miniature orchids). Trust me: you can't go wrong with mini orchids. Here are some simple ideas for decorating with them:

✤ Place in thimbles (miniature orchids can be very small), teacups, glasses, or silver salt and pepper shakers with the tops removed.

✤ Use dollhouse furniture to create a miniature setting: a little chair and table topped with a mini orchid.

✤ Place in apples, oranges, and smaller fruit (cut a tiny hole for the pot to fit) or among a mound of fruit.

✤ Attach name cards to the pots of miniature orchids with a hot-glue gun or double-sided tape.

Fragrance

An important but much-ignored factor in decorating with orchids is fragrance. In orchid shows in Japan, which has a very long history of orchid appreciation, there are special categories for scent alone. Scent can leave an impression greater than the orchid itself. Seek out fragrant orchids for your events, remembering that different ones are fragrant at different times of the day and night. I always factor in fragrance when choosing orchids for decorating. Try to find an orchid that works visually and also emits a wonderful scent.

For bedrooms, I obviously choose orchids that are fragrant at night, like angraecums, brassavola, and *Cattleya digbyana*. For kitchens, miltoniopsis, cattleyas, and day-fragrant oncidiums work well. In bathrooms, I go for orchids that are continuously fragrant like oncidium Sharry Baby and oncidium Twinkles (yes, those are their real names). When planning special events, choose orchids that are most fragrant during the time of the event. Give your guests the total orchid experience.

In this big orchid world you will be told that vandas and phalaenopsis are "never fragrant." Do not listen. There are many fragrant vandas and phalaenopsis, with more appearing each year as orchid growers notice the current trend.

My current favorite fragrant orchids are *Neofinetia falcata*, a small, easy-to-find fan-shaped species from Japan with a truly unique honeysuckle-like night fragrance, and *Cattleya Brassavola digbyana*, also easy to find and with a thick, sweet scent. A single neofinetia orchid will fill a room with fragrance. A single *Cattleya digbyana* will fill a house.

For a list of fragrant orchids, see page 137.

New miniature phalaenopsis are incredibly small—this photo shows a 1-inch pot.

*Oncidiums come in every size—note the miniature oncidium twinkles at the bottom
and the giant flowers at the top. These are a lovely choice for displaying in the home.*

A growing masdevallia hybrid surrounded by other orchids and epiphytes

J & L ORCHIDS
Easton, CT
203-261-3772
www.jlorchids.com

ORCHIDS BY HAUSERMANN
Villa Park, IL
630-543-6855
www.orchidsbyhausermann.com

ORCHIDS FOR THE PEOPLE
McKinleyville, CA
707-840-022
www.orchidpeople.com

SEATTLE ORCHID
Seattle, WA
877-380-6710
www.seattleorchid.com

WOODSTREAM ORCHIDS
Huntingtown, MD
410-286-2664
www.woodstreamorchids.com

VENDORS FOR HARDY ORCHIDS

Hardy orchids are orchids that have adapted to regional outdoor winter and summer temperatures, although the term is most commonly used for orchids found in regions with snow and freezing temperatures.

GARDENS AT POST HILL
860-567-0431
www.gardensatposthill.com

KEEPING IT GREEN NURSERY
360-652-1779
www.keepingitgreennursery.com

RAISING RARITIES.COM
419-866-4241
www.raisingrarities.com

VERMONT LADYSLIPPER COMPANY
www.vtladyslipper.com

WILD ORCHID COMPANY
215-297-0578
www.wildorchidcompany.com

INTERNATIONAL ORCHID SUPPLIERS

HANS CHRISTIANSEN ORCHIDEGARTNERIET
Fredensborg, Denmark
www.orchidegartneriet.dk

KLINGE ORCHIDEEN
Nederhorst den Berg, Netherlands
www.klinge.nl

MCBEAN'S ORCHIDS
Lewes, East Sussex, England
www.mcbeansorchids.co.uk

ORCHIDÉES VACHEROT ET LECOUFLE
Boissy-Saint-Léger, France
www.lorchidee.fr/

ORCHID HUB
Gerald Drive, Singapore
www.orchidhub.com

ORIENT Y ORCHIDS
Llambilles, Girona, Spain
www.orientyorchids.es

RATCLIFFE ORCHIDS LTD.
Owslebury, Winchester, England
www.ratcliffeorchids.co.uk

RIO VERDE ORQUIDEAS
Valle de Bravo, Edo., Mexico
www.orquideas.com

ROELLKE ORCHIDEEN
Stukenbrock, Germany
www.roellke-orchideen.de

ROYALE ORCHIDS
Peats Ridge, N. S. W., Australia
www.royaleorchids.com

RYANNE ORCHIDÉE
Bavay, France
www.ryanne-orchidee.com

SOBHA ORCHIDS
Kerala, India
www.sobhaorchids.com

ORCHID SUPPLIES

Here is a source guide for everything you need to grow orchids, from potting media to pots, fertilizers, shade cloth, and grow lights.

CHARLEY'S GREENHOUSE & GARDEN SUPPLY
Mount Vernon, WA
800-322-4707
www.charleysgreenhouse.com

KELLEY'S KORNER ORCHID SUPPLIES
Milford, NH
603-673-9524
www.kkorchid.com

ORCHID LIGHT.COM
Burlington, VT
800-261-3101
www.orchidlight.com

ORCHID SUPPLIES
Miami, FL
888-633-4685
www.ofe-intl.com

ORCHID SUPPLY.COM
Painesville, OH
888-437-0022
www.orchidsupply.com

REPOTME.COM
North Potomac, MD
301-315-2344
www.repotme.com

TOP FRAGRANT ORCHID
SPECIES AND HYBRIDS

Angraecum sesquipedale / The "Darwin orchid"; large flower, strong scent

Angraecum veitchii / A heavy, sweet nocturnal fragrance

Anguloa clowesii / The "tulip orchid"; strongly fragrant

Brassavola cucullata / A jasmine-honey scent

Brassavola digbyana / Incredibly strong night fragrance

Brassavola Little Stars / Very fragrant

Brassavola nodosa / The "lady of the night" orchid; super-sweet fragrance

Bulbophyllum species / Can be sweet-scented, but some species fetid

Catasetum species / All species sweetly scented

Cattleya bicolor / A strong daytime fragrance

Cattleya Bow Bells / A dependently fragrant hybrid

Cattleya schilleriana / A fresh late-morning fragrance

Cattleya Summer Stars / A fragrant white hybrid

Cymbidium dayanum / This species has a very clean, jasmine-like scent.

Cymbidium eburneum / All-day fragrance

Cymbidium tracyanum / My favorite cymbidium fragrance

Cycnoches egertonianum / Heavily fragrant "swan orchid"

Dendrobium anosmum / My favorite dendrobium fragrance; very strong

Dendrobium falcorostrum / Early afternoon fragrance

Dendrobium 'Gatton Sunray' / All-day citrus fragrance

Dendrobium kingianum / Uplifting morning fragrance

Encyclia fragrans / All "cockleshell" orchids have a wonderful daytime scent

Epidendrum parkinsonianum / Strong magnolia-meets-honeysuckle night scent

Epidendrum prismatocarpum / Unique sweet musky scent

Gongora species / All gongoras have a lovely daytime fragrance

Laelia crispa / Some clones incredibly fragrant

Laelia purpurata / National flower of Brazil: stunning large flowers with a fabulous scent

Laelia tenebrosa / A strong, pleasing fragrance

Lycaste aromatica / True to its name

Maxillaria tenuifolia / A strong cinnamon scent

Neofinetia falcata / The "wind," or "samurai" orchid: sweet fragrant white flowers

Oncidium cheirophorum / My favorite fragrant mini oncidium

Oncidium cucullatum / A citrus-like fragrance

Oncidium hastilabium / A strong afternoon fragrance

Oncidium lanceanum / Very sweet fragrant flowers

Oncidium leucochilum / Wonderfully fragrant hybrids

Oncidium ornithorhynchum / Most fragrant of oncidiums

Paphiopedilum delenatii / A soft rose scent

Paphiopedilum malipoense / A strong raspberry scent

Phalaenopsis lueddemanniana / Jasmine-like scent

Phalaenopsis mariae / A very sweet honey fragrance

Phalaenopsis Orchid World 'Sweet Fragrance' / Strongly fragrant hybrid

Phalaenopsis schilleriana / Some clones very fragrant

Phalaenopsis Sogo Rose 'Sweet Fragrance' / Intense berry scent

Phalaenopsis violacea / Berry-like scent

Sobralia fimbriata / A lovely narcissus scent

Vanda amesiana / Intense honeysuckle fragrance (my favorite)

Vanda tricolor / Strong, sweet daytime fragrance

Vanilla species / Vanilla scent

Wilsonara Jean DuPont / Some clones very fragrant

Zygopetalum Artur Elle / A nice floral scent

Zygopetalum blackii / A strong, sweet permeating scent

Zygopetalum mackayi / A strong hyacinth fragrance

Zygopetalum maxillare / A strong scent similar to narcissus

Disa, a South African terrestrial orchid, growing outside in San Francisco.

INDEX

Repotting, 30–32, 34–36, 51, 122
Rhizome, definition of, 12
Roots
    aerial, 11
    definition of, 12
    lack of, 17, 18, 35, 36
Rot, 46–47

S

Samples, 22
Scale, 45
Seedpod, definition of, 12
Sepals, definition of, 12
Sheath, definition of, 12
Sheet moss, 117
Shows, 21, 131, 134
Slat baskets, 43
Sobralia, 105
Societies, 19, 131
Spanish moss, 117
Species, definition of, 12
Sphagnum moss, 23, 31, 35, 37
Spider mites, 46
Stem support, 115
Sunrooms, 29
Sympodial orchids, 12, 47, 48

T

Terrestrial, definition of, 12
Travel tips, 37
Tree fern slabs, 42, 43–44
Tree trunks, mounting on, 43

V

Vanda, 19, 82–84
Vanilla orchid, 19, 99–101

W

Water, floating orchids in, 124, 125
Watering, 36–38, 48–49, 50–51
Wilsonara, 78
Windowsills, 28–29

Z

Zygopetalum, 105

ACKNOWLEDGMENTS

Thank you to every plant person who shared their knowledge and answered my questions throughout this process.

Thanks to my editor, Laura Lee Mattingly, for her patient and expert guidance and for her great attitude and sense of humor. Thanks to everyone at Chronicle Books for making this project possible.

Thanks to Greg Allikas for his hard work; to my good old friend and orchid comrade, Tom Perlite of Golden Gate Orchids; to the team at The Conservatory of Flowers—Brent Dennis, Jane Scurich, and Eric Imperial; Pui Chin, friend and legendary grower; Linda Haber, friend and windowsill orchid grower; Diane Murray, for making me look good; Cristina Marie for all the fun and help; and Ron Roselli my fellow grower.

A special thanks to Terry Root, partner at Oz Gardens; Hyman Fishman, partner at Rogers-Fishman Orchid Boarding; Kent Fujikawa, partner at Rogers-Fujikawa Orchids; and Mike Thompson, partner at Inflorescence.

Most of all, thank you to my friends and family for their unwavering support.